TELEVISION AND THE PUBLIC

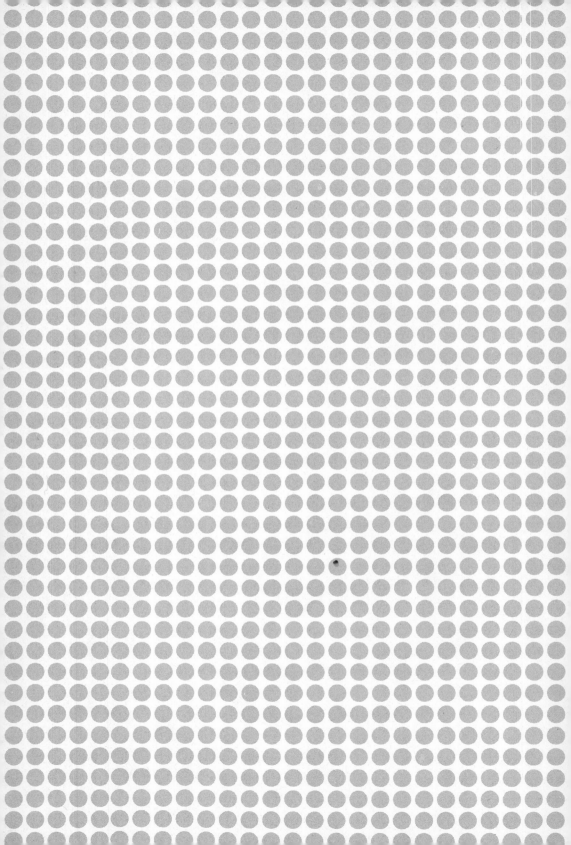

TELEVISION AND THE PUBLIC

ROBERT T. BOWER

HOLT, RINEHART AND WINSTON, INC.
New York   Chicago   San Francisco   Atlanta
Dallas   Montreal   Toronto   London   Sydney

Copyright © 1973 by Holt, Rinehart and Winston, Inc.
All rights reserved
Library of Congress Cataloging in Publication Data

Bower, Robert T
Television and the public.

1. Television audiences—United States.
2. Television broadcasting—United States.
I. Title
HE8700.7.A8B65   301.15'43'3875540973   73-3157
ISBN 0-03-008161-0
Printed in the United States of America
3456 038 987654321

PREFACE

In 1960, when Frank Stanton announced the Columbia Broadcasting System's support of an objective assessment of public reactions to television, he stated: "We owe it to our audience as well as ourselves to establish some systematic method of inviting the public to participate in shaping what we do." The public's participation was invited through a comprehensive sample survey of the U. S. adult population, carried out by the Bureau of Applied Social Research at Columbia University and reported in Dr. Gary Steiner's book *The People Look at Television: a Study of Audience Attitudes* (1963).

Steiner's inquiry provided the foundation for a second study ten years later, when the public was again invited to tell what they thought of television. Our main purpose in this second investigation was to see what might have happened during the decade to the public's attitudes toward the medium. Did viewers maintain the same level of regard for television? How did the changes that took place in television programming affect their attitudes? What did they see in television now that was rewarding or valuable or distressing that they had not seen a decade before?

This book, as Steiner's before it, draws upon a body of knowledge and experience in media research closely associated with the work of the Bureau of Applied Social Research. The Bureau's founder, Paul Lazarsfeld, began the systematic study of popular attitudes toward the mass media in the late 1930s, and the tradition has been maintained through such works as Lazarsfeld's *Radio and the Printed Page*, 1940; Lazarsfeld and Field's *The People Look at Radio*, 1946; and Katz and Lazarsfeld's *Personal Influence*, 1955. Gary Steiner's 1960 study of television lies squarely in that tradition, though he added some new techniques to his inquiry, such as the use of "semantic differential" word lists and projective questions. Much of what was asked about television in 1960 and again in 1970 is very similar to what was asked about radio in the 1940s, all in the abiding faith that the best way to find out what the people think about something is to ask them and, in doing so, to use the best methods of sampling and questioning that can be devised. This book draws heavily upon that tradition; it was patterned after the Steiner inquiry, repeating and elaborating on his research design. Beyond that intellectual debt, I am specifically grateful to BASR for turning over the code books, IBM cards, and computer tapes which permitted us to reexamine the 1960 study.

Most of the work on the present study was carried out at the Bureau of Social Science Research in Washington, D.C., with a great deal of help from my colleagues there. Samuel Meyers established the codes for some of the questionnaire items and set up the coding procedures for the 2335 completed questionnaires. Richard Jones shepherded the data through the computer. Ira Cisin worked with me in planning the analysis of the data and is responsible for the multivariate analyses that will be found in a few places in the book. Catherine Judd prepared some of the material on educational television and on the black audience. Ann Finkelstein was my chief collaborator. She prepared most of the tables in the report and drafted the chapter on Viewing in the Family.

The American Research Bureau provided television-watching diaries for a sample of households in Minneapolis–St. Paul which permitted comparisons between what people told our interviewers they liked and disliked about television with what they actually watched over a three-week period. An interesting dimension was added to the study because of this cooperation

The interviewing for the study, based on a national probability sample, was efficiently carried out by the field staff of the Roper Organization. Burns Roper, their president and Carolyn W. Crusius, their experienced field director provided indispensable technical assistance.

In supporting this second study through a grant to the Bureau of Social Science Research, CBS affirmed the investigator's right of control over all aspects of the inquiry, from the design of the study to the formulation and publication of the results. I am grateful for their abstention from even the faintest hint of self-serving interest in the way the study's results might fall, and for the professional help given by many members of their research staff. I am particularly appreciative of the generous assistance of David Blank, Vice President for Economics and Research of the CBS Broadcast Group, through which the grant was administered; and Joseph Klapper, Director of the Office of Social Research, himself one of our leading communications researchers.

Finally, my thanks to Professor W. Phillips Davison of Columbia University and Professor Harold Mendelsohn of the University of Denver who gave the manuscript a careful reading and suggested many improvements.

R.T.B.

Washington, D.C.
January 1973

CONTENTS

TELEVISION AND THE PUBLIC

CHAPTER 1

INTRODUCTION

When *The People Look at Television*[1] was published in 1963, it was hailed as the first comprehensive study of public reactions to the medium. The book was based on a 1960 survey for which a national cross-section of the United States' adult population was interviewed. These interviews were not only long in duration—two hours—but also broad in scope, covering peoples' television-viewing habits, their attitudes to the medium in general, their reactions to specific types of TV programs, their views about children's television-watching and attempts to control it, and a great deal of information about the characteristics of the interviewees themselves. Over three hundred questions were asked, some were in short checklist form, others permitted long, free answers. The study also included interviews among a special sample of New York City viewers, selected because they had previously filled out diaries recording a week's worth of television viewing; what they actually watched could be checked against what they said they liked.

It was indeed a comprehensive survey. With over 2700 interviews including those in New York; the sample was large enough to contain substantially large subgroups, and the questionnaire long enough to include

---

[1] Gary A. Steiner (New York: Alfred A. Knopf, 1963).

questions on almost everything one might want to know about reactions to television. Gary A. Steiner, who directed the study and wrote the book about it, was able to summarize the data from the interviews so that a broad picture of how people feel about television emerged; at the same time his analysis indicated the major differences of opinion among segments of the population and the differences in reaction to various types of television shows.

The population that Steiner studied in 1960 was found to have a high regard for television, in general. Television was perceived, then, primarily as an entertainment medium, offered to the public for their enjoyment and relaxation and embraced by most of them with pleasure and appreciation. Some were annoyed by the commercials, some found the quality of programs mediocre at best, some perceived harmful influences on children; but over all the fans far outnumbered the critics. The majority, for instance, thought that commercials were a fair price to pay for the advantages of television, and rated most of the programs they saw as enjoyable, rather than as "so-so" or "disappointing." An even larger majority thought that, in balance, children were better-off with television than without it.

This generally sanguine view was not shared equally among all segments of the 1960 population. People of higher socioeconomic status—the wealthier, better-educated, white-collar workers and professionals—were more apt to be critical of particular aspects of the medium and to think less of television in general. Steiner, in his report, concentrated particularly on the differences in points of view between the better and the less educated, choosing formal education as the key socioeconomic variable which separated critic from fan. Clearly, the college-educated men and women had most of the harsh things to say about television. But, strangely enough, the survey revealed that they tended to watch it much more than their views would indicate, and what they watched was rather similar to what everybody else was watching. Steiner saw a dissonance here between beliefs and actions that breeds a psychological dilemma. Indeed, he found that the higher educated tend to feel guilty about their TV viewing to a greater extent than do others.

The study reported here looks again at some of these earlier findings, through procedures closely following those used by Steiner. Ten years later, interviewers from The Roper Organization, which had conducted half the interviewing in the 1960 survey, were knocking on doors around the country in late winter and early spring, equipped with a questionnaire containing many of Steiner's queries. The basic sample was somewhat smaller, just 1900 persons 18-years old and older. Additional interviews were conducted among the 18- and 19-year olds, and a special survey was made in

Minneapolis—St. Paul among people who had filled out television-viewing diaries, replicating in intent Steiner's New York City study.

By the beginning of the sixties, the television set had become one of the more familiar objects in American households: nearly nine-tenths of all families had at least one set in working order. It was in the previous decade that the American home had been massively invaded by the new medium. During the 1950s the number of homes with television went from 4 million (9 percent of all homes) to 46 million (88 percent of all homes)—an expansion that even surpassed that of radio two decades before. By 1960, there were not many holdouts left and the rate of growth had slowed to less than one percent a year by 1970, when 95 percent of all American households had at least one set.

The big story of the sixties for the television industry is not its capture of the living room. Having nearly achieved that, it followed a familiar consumer-goods pattern—once the market approaches saturation with the first model of a product, the next stage of expansion lies in the purchase of the second and in substitutions of improved models for the old. Consider the push-button telephone, the transistor radio, or the second automobile. Color television sets, just becoming available in 1960, found their way into over a third of the American households by 1970. The proportion of homes with sets equipped for reception of ultra-high frequency channels went from 8 percent to 63 percent (following a 1962 federal regulation requiring that all new sets be so equipped after April 1964). The number of households with more than one set nearly tripled, so that by 1970, 31 percent of all TV households had two or more sets. Our survey found 11 percent with *three* or more.

While the public was acquiring more and better television sets, the broadcasting industry was embarking on a parallel expansion. The number of commercial broadcasting stations using VHF increased somewhat from 440 to 508, while the UHF stations went from 75 to over 180. There were 44 noncommercial educational stations on the air in 1960 and 184 in 1970, with the largest increase among the UHF stations.

Over the decade, the increase in the number of households hooked to a cable television system went from virtually zero to 8 percent. The growth of CATV systems from 640 to 2350 was predominantly in the geographically isolated areas—those with very poor reception or none at all—but some of the new systems were also established in large and medium-sized cities with relatively good reception. New York City, for instance, now has three competing cable systems and the Federal Communications Commission has so far issued twenty licenses for Los Angeles County (Table 1-1).

3

table 1-1
Growth in the Television Industry

	1960	1970
NUMBER OF STATIONS AND SYSTEMS IN OPERATION		
Commercial TV		
UHF	75	183
VHF	440	508
Educational TV		
UHF	10	106
VHF	34	78
CATV Systems	640	2350
TELEVISION HOUSEHOLD DATA		
Number of sets in use	53 million	88 million
Percent of all households with TV	87.5	95.5
Percent of all households with color TV	*	40**
Percent of TV households with two or more sets .	12.5	30.5
Percent of TV sets equipped for UHF	8	52
Percent of households subscribing to CATV	*	7.5

* Less than one percent.
** Based on estimates from *Electronic Market Data Book*, Nielsen data, and 1970 survey findings.
Sources: United States Census; *Dimensions of Television, 1970; Television Factbook, 1970-1971;* and Nielsen data.

These various changes during the sixties suggested some obvious additions to the Steiner inquiry; we added questions about CATV, color television and educational television, and concerned ourselves with the influence the extra sets might have on family viewing.

There were also some significant changes in the composition of the U.S. population during the decade, some of which are shown in Table 1-2.

One of the more notable shifts is the increase in the proportion of the 18- to 24-year-old group; there were 7,625,000 more persons in this group in 1970 than in 1960. These young adults are the products of the post-World War II "Baby Boom." Since 1960, the proportion of the total population in this age category has averaged an annual increase of 4.2

table 1-2
Population Shifts in the U.S. (in percentages)

	1960	1970
AGE (Base: Persons Aged 18 and Over)		

AGE	1960	1970
18–19	4.2 ⎱ 23.2	5.6 ⎱ 28.0
20–29	19.0 ⎰	22.4 ⎰
30–39	21.2 ⎱ 40.7	16.9 ⎱ 35.0
40–49	19.5 ⎰	18.1 ⎰
50–59	15.6 ⎱	15.8 ⎱
60–64	6.1 ⎰ 36.0	6.4 ⎰ 37.1
65 and over	14.3 ⎰	14.9 ⎰

YEARS OF EDUCATION (Base: Persons Aged 18 and Over)

	1960	1970
0–4	7.5	4.5
5–8	28.6	19.4
9–11	20.2	17.8
12	26.7 ⎱	35.7 ⎱
1–2 college	7.8 ⎰ 43.5	11.8 ⎰ 59.9
3–4 years college and over	9.0 ⎰	12.4 ⎰

SEX (Base: Persons Aged 18 and Over)

	1960	1970
Males	48.3	47.5
Females	51.7	52.5

RACE (Base: Persons Aged 18 and Over)

	1960	1970
White	89.8	88.9
Negro	9.4	9.8
Other	0.8	1.3

OCCUPATION (Base: Persons 14 and Over) — (Base: Persons 16 and Over)

	1960 (Base: Persons 14 and Over)	1970 (Base: Persons 16 and Over)
White collar	43.1	48.6
Blue collar	56.9	51.4

GEOGRAPHICAL DISTRIBUTION (Base: Total Population)

	1960	1970
Urban	69.9	73.5
Rural	30.1	26.5

Source: United States Census.

percent, compared to an average annual total population increase of 1.3 percent over the same time period. A much smaller relative increase has taken place in the older age categories, the result primarily of greater longevity in our society. The middle group, 30- to 40-years old, has declined in relative terms. This table also shows a clear, over-all trend toward a more highly educated public over the ten-year period. Some of the more significant figures indicate that 24.2 percent of the 1970 population have at least some college experience, as compared to 16.8 percent in 1960; those receiving a high school diploma have increased from 43.5 percent in 1960 to 59.9 percent in 1970.

Many of these ten-year changes could affect the way the public feels about television. There are more and better sets around, more of them with color pictures and many more equipped to receive UHF channels; there are more broadcasting stations on the air. We could expect, therefore, that people might react to these improvements by responding more favorably than they had ten years before to questions about the medium. On the other hand, some changes in the composition of the population could lead to an opposite assumption. It is known that the higher-educated members of the population tend to be less enthusiastic about television—Steiner's study and many others since have shown that to be true. With the whole population becoming better educated, one might expect an increasing number of people with critical attitudes.

In addition to expansion of the industry and the altered composition of the population, there were changes in the content of the medium which must be taken into account. New entertainment programs came on the air and old ones disappeared; the journalistic role of television became more prominent with live and on-the-spot coverage of national and international events—including the first televised war—and with more prime viewing time devoted to them. More full-length movies could be found in the evening hours and longer coverage of sports events on weekends, while the number of westerns decreased. Negroes appeared on the screen in significant entertainment roles and as local newscasters, and broadcasting station representatives started presenting editorial opinions on current issues. There was not as much over-all change in typical programming, even with the increase of educational television stations, as some of the critics would have liked; but there was certainly enough new content over the ten year period to permit conjecture as to its effects on popular attitudes.

A cautionary note should be sounded. It would be a mistake to assume that reactions to television can be fully explained by television itself. To begin with, television is not a readily definable unitary element, like the isolated stimulus in a psychological experiment. TV can be *Beverly Hillbillies* to one person, the Vietnam War to a second and the *Superbowl* to a third. Also, reliance on the medium for entertainment or for information may vary according to peoples' life circumstances—a necessary link to the outside world for the widower or a neglected piece of furniture for the popular single girl. Furthermore, television may be used by anyone at various times in various ways—as an escape from overindulgence in thought, as a way to keep the children pacified, as a means to keep up with the affairs of the world or perhaps as the center of conviviality of the family group that sits before the set on a winter evening. Its intellectual, psychological, and social functions are myriad.

One further qualification: attitudes toward television, or toward anything else for that matter, are subject to influences from the social milieu in which the individual grows up and lives. Views that are acceptable on Beacon Hill may not be so in Haight-Asbury. In sociological parlance, the question "is television wonderful or terrible?" may be mentally submitted to different sets of reference groups for mediation before the answer is given to the interviewer.

At best, then, the content of television can only be a partial explanation of the attitudes that people have toward it, at any point in time. And if attitudes appear to have changed over a ten-year period, we cannot assume that the changes can be attributed entirely to the ways in which television has changed. Many other influences may be at work.

In the 1970 survey we used about a third of the questions that were asked in 1960, choosing those that appeared to tap important aspects of the public reactions to television and which, secondly, did not present severe methodological difficulties in their replication. Many open-ended questions that allowed for long answers in varieties of thematic dimensions were rejected. They were good questions, but it would have been almost impossible to classify the answers with the assurance that the judgment of our classifiers matched those of Steiner, rendering dubious any quantitative ten-year comparisons. For purposes of replication, a simple checklist type of question is preferable. The Steiner questions we did select were asked in precisely the same words and in the same sequence in the questionnaire. Enough was passed over of the previous questionnaire to permit additions directed toward new features of television in the seventies and new issues that had arisen about the medium. The 1970 questionnaire expanded Steiner's coverage of educational television and of the role of television journalism. We also dealt more extensively with decision-making in the choice of programs, especially in the family setting.

The present study also differs slightly from the previous one in the sampling procedures employed. Steiner had used two national area samples with interviewers, respectively, from the National Opinion Research Center and Elmo Roper and Associates. Within chosen geographic areas, the interviewers selected respondents, 18-years old and older, to fill established quotas—so many within each age–sex stratum. The Roper Organization, which carried out the 1970 field work, used a standard area probability sample, with four attempts to interview each designated respondent; the number of call-backs was subsequently increased in areas of exceptionally low yield. The 18- and 19-year olds were oversampled in the hope that we would end up with enough of them for separate analysis. A total of 1991 people were interviewed. When the cases were weighted to adjust for the oversupply of teen-agers, the final number for analysis was just 1900. The sampling procedures are described in detail in the Appendix, along with a comparison of the final results and the 1970 data on the United States population as a whole.

Procedures standard to the age of computers were used in processing the data and in the analysis. The only deviation from the most ordinary of statistical techniques is the use, here and there, of a computer program for multivariate analysis sometimes known as the Automatic Interaction Detection (AID) technique developed first by the English social scientist William Belson and later elaborated at the University of Michigan. Otherwise, the data are presented in percentaged tables and charts. Since tests of significance are not included in the tables, the reader may wish to consult the Appendix note on Statistical Measures.[2]

We should note also that this book lacks the comprehensive bibliography that usually adorns such works. A vast amount of literature has been published since 1960 about television. Here and there we cite some other relevant works, but our main source for comparisons is Steiner and that is where we have looked primarily for supporting and conflicting results. Fortunately, two excellent bibliographies are available for the scholar who will notice the lack of any comprehensive review of the literature in this work. Leo Bogart's third edition of *The Age of Television*[3] contains an up-to-date literature review and a bibliography of over 400 items; and a 150-page annotated bibliography was brought out in 1971 under the aegis of the U. S. Surgeon General's Scientific Advisory Committee on Television and Social Behavior.[4]

The journey through the data starts in Chapter 2, with an overview of the broad changes in attitude toward television during the ten years

---

[2] For explanations of the procedures used in data analysis throughout this book see Appendix C.

[3] Leo Bogart, *The Age of Television*, 3d ed., New York: Frederick Ungar Publishing Co., 1972.

[4] Charles K. Atkin, John P. Murray, and Oguz B. Nayman, eds., *Television And Social Behavior, an Annotated Bibliography*, Washington, D.C.: Government Printing Office, PHS Publication No. 2099, 1971.

that separate the two surveys. Chapter 3 deals with the characteristics of television's audience and the factors that seem to affect the amount of time people spend in viewing. We then, in Chapter 4, examine the public's reactions to various sorts of programming, its perceptions and evaluations of the changes that have taken place in television's content. Chapter 5 singles out one variety of content—television news—that has assumed sufficient prominence in the public's view of the medium to justify separate treatment.

Chapter 6 draws upon the results of the special study in Minneapolis—St. Paul to compare what people have been telling us about their preferences with what they actually watch, and Chapter 7 deals with the dynamics of television viewing within the family and with parents' attitudes about their children's viewing. The concluding chapter attempts to tie together some of the loose ends.

CHAPTER 2
TEN-YEAR ATTITUDE CHANGES

On the cover of a recent British book about television, there is a picture of a family gathered in the living room watching a program: the father is snoozing, his son weeping, his wife laughing, while his brother has a quizzical frown. Could an American publisher truthfully depict such diverse reactions to a television show?

Gary Steiner's most sweeping conclusion from his 1960 survey of American reactions was that "the general viewer feels generally good about television in general." The statement suggests more of a consensus than the disparity found in the British living-room scene. However, another Steiner conclusion was that what is true for people *in general* does not apply equally to all types of viewers, and that some aspects of television elicit more favorable reactions than others. These broad statements might also be made with qualifications about 1970 television audiences. In 1970, as in 1960, people are generally favorable toward television and differ from one another in their views about different television content. In addition, over the course of the decade people have changed their views of television, some more than others.

This chapter examines, at a very broad attitudinal level, the public's view of television and the changes in that viewpoint during ten years. We will first deal with aggregate attitude trends of the American public as a whole, and then shift to examine various groups in the population as they agree or differ with one another.

To present such a broad profile of change in attitudes about television over the decade, every effort was made in 1970 to replicate precisely the Steiner study—not only the questions but also the interviewer's procedures in asking them and the sequential order of the questions in the course of the interview. We started this inquiry, as did Steiner, with a few background questions about consumer items in general which were asked before the interview concentrated on television almost exclusively. The answers to these introductory questions are shown in Table 2-1.

When we asked our respondents which of five items they could not live without for a few months, we found that automobiles and refrigerators are considered to be the greatest necessities of life. Only 5 percent in both 1960 and 1970 chose television for the three-month survival kit and not too many more added it as their second or third choice. To find that there are some goods and services more vital and more highly regarded than television may not be the greatest of surprises, but it is at least chastening; it lends an initial perspective to the investigation of a medium which has penetrated practically every American home, which absorbs more of our waking hours than any single pursuit other than work, and which is the subject of so much concentrated research, discussion, and controversy.

Television, as a goods and service designed to please the public, came in second to automobiles in both 1960 and 1970. The more recent study shows, furthermore, that television has suffered a decline as a satisfying service, relative to the other items, from 29 percent to 16 percent of the first choices. It might be noted also that the only other mass medium of communication listed—the press—fares worse in 1970 than in 1960 as a necessity in short-term survival. First choices for newspapers declined from 11 to 5 percent, while television at least protected its modest claim to one-twentieth of the first choices.

A third set of ten-year comparisons can be seen in Table 2-2 which shows the answers to a series of questions in which people were asked to choose among four mass media of communication on a variety of dimensions.

At the time of Steiner's study, each of the media received a decisive plurality of the choices on at least one of the comparisons. Television was felt to be the most entertaining, it created the most interest in new things going on, and it seemed to be getting better all the time; radio brought the latest news most quickly; newspapers gave the most complete news coverage and did the most for the public. Magazines got their pluralities of the votes on losing tickets—as "the least important" medium which

table 2-1

"Here are some things that many people take for granted today. But imagine, if you can, that for two or three months you could have only one of these and you'd have to do without the rest.

"If you could only have one of those things, which one would you choose? What would be the second, third item you'd want?"

	1st Choice		2nd Choice		3rd Choice	
PERCENT WHO SAY:						
	1960	1970	1960	1970	1960	1970
Refrigerator	38	38	24	31	15	16
Automobile	31	41	28	28	17	13
Newspaper	11	5	12	8	16	13
Telephone	10	11	21	22	27	34
Television	5	5	14	11	24	24
Don't know, NA	5	1	1	0	1	1

"Here is another list of five different products and services designed to please the general public.

"With which of these five things are you personally most satisfied; your second choice?"

	1st Choice		2nd Choice	
PERCENT WHO SAY:				
	1960	1970	1960	1970
Automobiles	48	50	24	19
Television programs	29	16	36	32
Fashions for women	11	15	13	17
Popular music	7	7	11	14
Movies	2	3	8	6
None, NA and DK	3	8	8	11

1960 base: 100 percent = 2427
1970 base: 100 percent = 1900

13

table 2-2

"Now, I would like to get your opinions about how radio, newspapers, television, and magazines compare. Generally speaking, which of these would you say . . .?"

IN PERCENTAGES

WHICH OF THE MEDIA:	TELEVISION 1960	1970	MAGAZINES 1960	1970	NEWSPAPERS 1960	1970	RADIO 1960	1970	NONE/NA 1960	1970
Is the most entertaining?	68	72	9	5	13	9	9	14	1	0
Gives the most complete news coverage?	19	41	3	4	59	39	18	14	1	2
Presents things most intelligently?	27	38	27	18	33	28	8	9	5	8
Is the most educational?	32	46	31	20	31	26	3	4	3	5
Brings you the latest news most quickly?	36	54	0	0	5	6	57	39	2	1
Does the most for the public?	34	48	3	2	44	28	11	13	8	10
Seems to be getting worse all the time?	24	41	17	18	10	14	14	5	35	22
Presents the fairest, most unbiased news?	29	33	9	9	31	23	22	19	9	16
Is the least important to you?	15	13	49	53	7	9	15	20	7	5
Creates the most interest in new things going on?	56	61	18	16	18	14	4	5	4	5
Does the least for the public?	13	10	47	50	5	7	12	13	23	20
Seems to be getting better all the time?	49	38	11	8	11	11	10	15	19	28
Gives you the clearest understanding of the candidates and issues in national elections?	42	59	10	8	36	21	5	3	7	9

1960 base: 100 percent = 2427
1970 base: 100 percent = 1900

14

"does the least for the public." Over all, television came out ahead of the other media in five of the ten items stated in positive terms. In two of the negatively stated items ("least important to you" and "does least for the public") it lost to magazines by a large margin. In response to the third negative item, there were more people who thought television was "getting worse all the time" (24 percent) than thought that of any of the other media, but there were even more—35 percent—who said that *none* of the media was getting worse all the time. Over all, it was a high but not entirely one-sided rating for television.

In 1970 an oddly altered picture emerges. Now, ten years later, television is chosen ahead of the three other media on *all ten* of the positive items. Not only is it still the most entertaining, educational, interest-creating, politically informative medium, and the one that is improving all the time; it also, says a plurality, brings information quicker, more completely, more intelligently and with less bias, and it does the most for the public.

But while this positive evaluation of TV in its identifiable functions—to entertain, to educate, to inform—is advancing, there also seems to be an increase in *negative* evaluations on less specific items. As the medium that "is getting worse all the time," television *increases* from 24 to 41 percent; as the medium which is "getting better" its vote *decreases* from 49 to 38 percent. More people now think that television is getting worse than think that it is improving. Previously the balance was tilted on the side of improvement. This is a marked negative shift from the 1960 views, a shift that is taking place at the same time that an increasing number of people are giving television a high performance rating on other dimensions.

These appear to be contradictory trends if one assumes some law of consistency among all the elements that may make up a summarized, aggregated view of the public toward a subject such as television. But such apparent inconsistencies are frequently found in attitude research. To take an example from another area entirely, studies have shown that people tend to express punitive, repressive views when asked in a general way about America's crime problem and how to solve it, but they express more lenient views when asked what should be done in the hypothetical case of a boy caught stealing a car.[1] The general and the specific questions evoke opposite attitudinal responses. In the same way we find that different elements of peoples' views on television are going in opposite directions simultaneously. While the more general attitudes about television—which the questions on "getting better," and "getting worse" might tap—are declin-

---

[1] U. S. President's Commission on Law Enforcement and the Administration of Justice *Crime and Its Impact: An Assessment*, Washington, D.C., 1970, pp. 90–91.

table 2-3a

"Here are some opposites. Please read each pair quickly and put a check some place between them, wherever you think it belongs to describe television. Just your offhand impression."

TELEVISION IS GENERALLY: Proportion of 1960-1970 samples choosing each of six scale positions

	(1)		(2)		(3)		(4)		(5)		(6)		
	1960	1970	1960	1970	1960	1970	1960	1970	1960	1970	1960	1970	
Relaxing	43	33	21	23	19	27	9	11	3	4	4	3	Upsetting
Interesting	42	31	21	23	19	24	9	13	4	5	4	3	Uninteresting
For Me	41	27	16	20	19	24	10	15	6	8	8	6	Not for me
Important	39	30	17	19	21	24	10	15	7	7	6	6	Unimportant
Informative	39	35	25	27	20	23	8	9	5	3	3	3	Not informative
Lots of fun	32	22	20	20	25	31	12	16	5	6	6	5	Not much fun
Exciting	30	19	18	17	29	35	13	17	5	7	4	6	Dull
Wonderful	28	19	16	15	33	36	16	22	4	6	3	3	Terrible
Imaginative	26	19	21	20	28	33	14	15	6	7	5	6	No imagination
In good taste	24	18	21	19	31	33	19	19	6	7	4	4	In bad taste
Generally excellent	22	15	19	18	32	36	18	21	5	6	4	4	Generally bad
Average of Eleven Items	33	24	20	20	25	30	13	16	5	6	5	4	

1960 Base: 100 percent = 2427
1970 Base: 100 percent = 1900

table 2-3b

"Here are some opposites. Please read each pair quickly and put a check some place between them, wherever you think it belongs to describe television. Just your offhand impression."

TELEVISION IS GENERALLY: Proportion of 1960-1970 samples choosing each of six scale positions

	(1)		(2)		(3)		(4)		(5)		(6)		
	1960	1970	1960	1970	1960	1970	1960	1970	1960	1970	1960	1970	
Lots of variety	35	28	16	20	19	21	12	14	10	9	8	8	All the same
On everyone's mind	33	21	22	18	24	29	15	20	4	7	3	5	Nobody cares much
Getting better	25	16	19	15	24	23	16	21	8	11	9	15	Getting worse
Keeps changing	23	22	17	18	22	24	18	20	10	9	9	8	Stays the same
Serious	8	7	8	8	31	35	29	33	12	10	12	7	Playful
Too "highbrow"	4	3	3	4	29	28	42	43	11	12	9	11	Too "simple minded"
Average of Six Items	21	16	14	14	25	27	21	25	9	8	8	9	

1960 Base: 100 percent = 2427
1970 Base: 100 percent = 1900
(Excluding NA's which vary from item to item)

17

ing, there is an increased appreciation of some particular tasks that the medium performs—like bringing the news.

That there may be broad, general attitudes toward television which can be distinguished from more specific views leads immediately to a third set of data. In both 1960 and 1970, the respondent was asked to check the position on a series of scales which he thought best "describes" television. If he thought it *very* exciting he would check a box far to the left, if *very* dull his check would be on the far right; if he thought it somewhere in between, that's where his check mark would be. The intent was to get a rapid first-blush reaction to the medium, in response to "semantic differential" items, which in summary represent an attitudinal profile of television.

Table 2-3a shows the 1960 and 1970 responses to some items which are clearly directional—favorable to television at one end and unfavorable on the other. Compared to ten years ago, television is now *less* exciting, *less* interesting, *less* wonderful, *less* everything good. In 2-3b, though not as pronounced, the trend is in an over-all negative direction, assuming that our terms are properly arranged. We assume that "keeps changing" is a more favorable view than "stays the same." For some people it may not be.

The direction of the trend is both clear and consistent with the earlier findings—that television has declined in comparison with other goods and services which people are "most satisfied with," and that, in comparison with other media, more people now than before think television is getting worse. The table also tells us something about the *extent* of the shift. People are not leaping in droves from a feeling that television is "wonderful" to a feeling that it is "terrible." They are merely slipping down the scale a bit from a quite high evaluation to a somewhat lower one. Note that the extreme right-hand (unfavorable) side has hardly changed at all and that while the ranks of the most-favorable position on the left have been depleted, it is the middle positions that have gained. A trend indeed, but no violent upheaval in the public's attitude toward the medium.

In order to provide a summary "attitude score" for the 1960 and 1970 populations, we selected seven of the items in the "semantic differential" battery which served unambiguously to tap negative or positive feelings about television (television is—exciting–dull; important–unimportant; generally excellent–generally bad; in good taste–in bad taste; interesting–uninteresting; wonderful–terrible; for me–not for me). The response to each item could receive a score of zero for the most negative position on up to five for the most positive; so on all seven items combined, the scores ranged from zero for the uncompromising despiser of television to 35 for the extreme enthusiast. In 1960 the average score for the whole population was 24 out of the maximum of 35; by 1970 it had dropped to 22.

As representing very broad and general attitudes toward television, these scores were used at various points in the treatment of the data for both years. In the first instance, they provide the criterion measure for an analysis of the background factors that may influence attitudes when their various interrelationships are taken into account.

From the 1960 data we have information on eleven factors, each of which might theoretically have some effect on how people feel about television—sex, age, education, race, occupation, income, the presence or absence of children in the household, religion, political preference, region of the country and the size of the place in which the respondent lives—from large cities to rural areas. In 1970 we could add a twelfth—the respondent's leaning toward liberalism or conservatism. Those factors—all potential "predictors" of attitudes—were subjected to a multivariate analysis by means of the computerized "Automatic Interaction Detection" (AID) program, which in effect allows one to see which among the factors are most closely related to attitudes even though they may be interrelated themselves (Charts 2-1 and 2-2). People with higher family incomes are apt to be better educated than people from poorer families. Is it income or education that would better predict how a person would feel about television?

The results of the AID analysis can be displayed in the form of upside-down family trees, as shown in Charts 2-1 and 2-2. At the top is the total sample; next below is a split of the sample by that factor which best discriminates between the higher and the lower attitudes (in statistical terms, the factor that explains more of the total variance than any other). As we go further down on the branches, the factors become less important as predictors of attitudes.

In 1960, four factors survived the statistical tests that were employed in order to eliminate background factors whose contribution to the total explained variance was negligible. Education, race, income, and political affiliation all showed some relationship to attitudes, with the first two carrying most of the weight. In 1970 race and education, in that order, again appear as the dominant factors, with region of the country playing a minor part among the middle-educated white viewers and age appearing as a factor among the less educated. The terminal groups can be placed in order by their average attitude scores, from high to low, as in Table 2-4.

In 1960, blacks with no more than a high school education held the most favorable attitude toward television and the college-educated whites with moderate or high income the lowest. In 1970 blacks were again on top, regardless of education or other factors and college-educated whites at the bottom. It is interesting to note two factors that do *not* emerge from the analysis. Women, who make up the bulk of television's daytime audience, apparently do not differ much from men in their general atti-

19

chart 2-1
1960 Attitude Scores

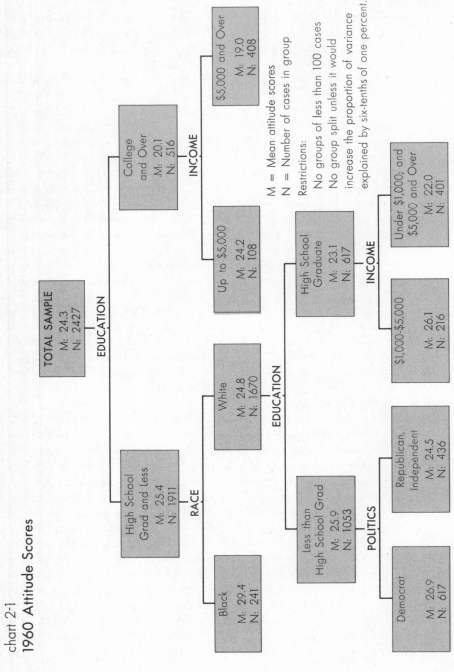

TOTAL SAMPLE
M: 24.3
N: 2427

EDUCATION

College and Over
M: 20.1
N: 516

High School Grad and Less
M: 25.4
N: 1911

INCOME

$5,000 and Over
M: 19.0
N: 408

Up to $5,000
M: 24.2
N: 108

RACE

White
M: 24.8
N: 1670

Black
M: 29.4
N: 241

EDUCATION

High School Graduate
M: 23.1
N: 617

Less than High School Grad
M: 25.9
N: 1053

INCOME

Under $1,000, and $5,000 and Over
M: 22.0
N: 401

$1,000-$5,000
M: 26.1
N: 216

POLITICS

Republican, Independent
M: 24.5
N: 436

Democrat
M: 26.9
N: 617

M = Mean attitude scores
N = Number of cases in group
Restrictions:
No groups of less than 100 cases
No group split unless it would increase the proportion of variance explained by six-tenths of one percent.

chart 2-2
1970 Attitude Scores

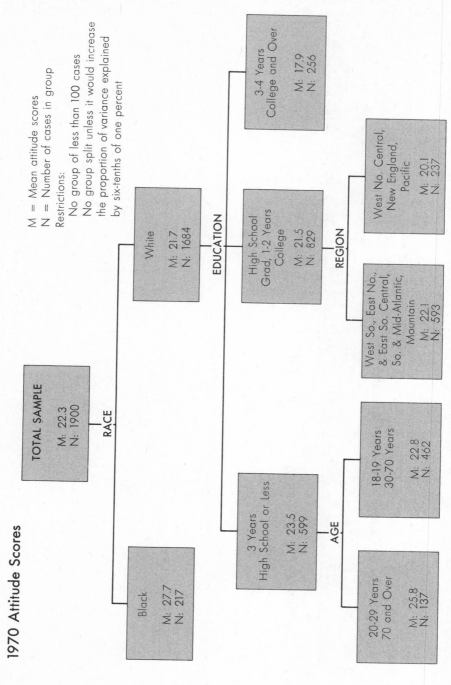

M = Mean attitude scores
N = Number of cases in group
Restrictions:
No group of less than 100 cases
No group split unless it would increase
the proportion of variance explained
by six-tenths of one percent

TOTAL SAMPLE

M: 22.3
N: 1900

RACE

White

M: 21.7
N: 1684

Black

M: 27.7
N: 217

EDUCATION

3-4 Years
College and Over

M: 17.9
N: 256

High School
Grad, 1-2 Years
College

M: 21.5
N: 829

3 Years
High School or Less

M: 23.5
N: 599

REGION

West No. Central,
New England,
Pacific

M: 20.1
N: 237

West So., East No.,
& East So. Central,
So. & Mid-Atlantic,
Mountain

M: 22.1
N: 593

AGE

18-19 Years
30-70 Years

M: 22.8
N: 462

20-29 Years
70 and Over

M: 25.8
N: 137

table 2-4
Attitude Scores by Combined Group Characteristics

1960

EDUCATION	RACE	INCOME	POLITICS	ATTITUDE SCORE	BASE: 100% =
High School graduate and less	Black	—	—	29.4	241
Less than High School graduate	White	—	Democrat	26.9	617
Less than High School graduate	White	—	Republican or Independent	24.5	436
College	—	Up to $5,000	—	24.2	108
High School Graduate	White	$1,000–5,000	—	23.1	216
High School Graduate	White	Under $1,000 & over $5,000	—	22.0	401
College	—	Over $5,000	—	19.0	408

1970

EDUCATION	RACE	AGE	REGION	ATTITUDE SCORE	BASE: 100% =
Three years High School or less	Black	—	—	27.7	228
Three years High School or less	White	20–29 & 70–79	—	25.8	137
	White	18–19 & 30–70	East Central & West South Central	22.8	486
High School Graduate & 1-2 years College	White	—	Southern & Mid-Atlantic Mountain New England	22.1	633
High School Graduate & 1-2 years College	White	—	West North Central Pacific	20.1	251
Three years College & above	White	—	—	17.9	256

tudes toward the medium, and parents of children under 15, whom one might imagine to be influenced, positively or negatively, by the presence of an avid TV fan in the house, do not differ from the others.

This analysis chiefly serves to identify two factors—the amount of education and race—that would appear to have been important determinants of general attitudes in both 1960 and 1970. Some of the characteristics of the black audience will be treated in the next chapter and education will be dealt with as a variable to help illuminate various findings throughout the report.

SUPERFANS AND VILIFIERS

Before leaving this sketch of the ten-year downward trend in generalized attitudes toward television, we should return to one component of that trend which was noted above but then became submerged in the summary attitude scores. The shifts seemed to come largely from the favorable end of the scale. Those people who checked the most extremely favorable position and those who were as negative as the scale would allow are worth some attention. The items are highly intercorrelated—the person who checked an extremely favorable or unfavorable position on one item was apt to check the same way on many of the others. Two of the items, television is "wonderful"–"terrible" and it is "for me"–"not for me," may be used as examples to examine the characteristics of these superfans and vilifiers (Table 2-5).

In 1960, there were superfans among men and women equally. Steiner, indeed, comments in his book on the amazing similarity between the sexes in the proportions having extremely favorable attitudes toward the medium. However, differences were found among other variables. There were many more 1960 superfans among the grade-school population than among the college-educated. To a lesser degree, the two ends of the age distribution—the teen-agers and the over sixties—tended to have more highly enthusiastic viewers than the ages in between.

By 1970, each of the groups had lost a considerable number of its superfans—some of them more than others. The men, for example, became less enthusiastic about TV than the women, and the teen-age population lost a slightly higher proportion of its enthusiasts than the other age groups. The composite picture of the 1970 superfan is thus altered slightly from its counterpart of a decade earlier, showing a slightly older and more feminine profile.

More significant than these small changes in the composite picture is the finding that the extremely large number of superfans that Steiner

table 2-5

Proportion of Each Group Taking Most Extreme Positions on Two Scales

| | SUPERFANS PERCENT WHO CHECK EXTREME POSITIVE POSITION | | | | VILIFIERS PERCENT WHO CHECK EXTREME NEGATIVE POSITIONS | | | | BASE: 100% = | |
| | "WONDERFUL" | | "FOR ME" | | "TERRIBLE" | | "NOT FOR ME" | | | |
	1960	1970	1960	1970	1960	1970	1960	1970	1960	1970
Sex:										
Male	27	17	40	24	3	4	7	7	1177	900
Female	28	20	41	31	3	2	9	6	1246	982
Education:										
Grade School	33		54	43	3	3	9	7	627	367
High School	26	19	42	28	3	3	7	6	1214	1030
College	12	7	20	15	3	2	11	8	516	490
Age:										
18–19	32	17	44	25	0	2	6	7	84	182
20–29	19	17	33	29	3	1	8	6	473	331
30–39	23	18	39	24	2	3	7	6	544	356
40–49	27	13	38	23	2	3	7	9	463	378
50–59	34	21	44	27	4	2	10	5	400	311
60+	36	24	50	33	4	5	10	6	440	419

25

found has declined across the board, among all groups. One is tempted, immediately, to look for an explanation by examining the medium—what has happened to television over the decade that it should lose so many of its extreme adherents? However, to anticipate a later finding, popular re-action to most of the changes in the medium has largely been favorable; an issue we will examine in a subsequent chapter. The sheer size of the superfan group in 1960 suggests an alternative explanation; it seems almost too big to be real. Perhaps enthusiasm for television was at an exceptionally high point in 1960 because many people were still reacting with awe to the new electronic gadget in the living room, a new and wonderful source of entertainment and relaxation, like the first week with the birthday bike. The rapid rise in television ownership in the fifties, followed by its snail's pace advance in the sixties, means that for many more families at the time of the first study, television was indeed an innovation. Perhaps the ardor of the love affair was temporized by the passage of time and by daily con-tact with the set; it has now settled into a moderate affection that permits people to view that object with a more discriminating eye. There have been some speculations along these lines by social researchers. Lo Sciuto, for instance, suggests that ". . . as television continues to grow in familiarity, its use is likely to excite fewer feelings either for or against it among the viewing public,"[2] and pollster Louis Harris adds a further dimension when he points out that Americans are becoming increasingly critical of many of our institutions, including the mass media.[3]

At the other end of the scale, where we find a small group of all-out television-haters (a possible 5 or 6 percent of the population) no pattern at all emerges. They were apt to come from any segment of the population in 1960 and again in 1970. They can be old or young, male or female, uneducated or highly educated. The lack of any clear relationship between demographic characteristics of the population and choice of the most anti-television position suggests that the genesis of the extremely negative attitude may lie more in the individual psychology or the unique life experi-ences of the viewers than in their social characteristics. It is not, in any case, a group that is definable by the data we collected in this study.

The broad ten-year trends that have been observed in this section provide a starting point for much of the discussion which follows. While general attitudes favoring television were declining, more people than

---

[2] Leonard Lo Sciuto, "Inventory of Television Viewing Behavior," in *Television and Social Behavior*, A Technical Report to the Surgeon General's Scientific Advisory Com-mittee on Television and Social Behavior, Washington, D.C.: 1972.

[3] Louis Harris, address before the American Newspaper Publishers Association meeting, published in *Editor and Publisher*, May 20, 1972, p. 6.

before were giving television a high rating as a news medium, leading us to a more detailed review of the journalistic functions of television. The characteristics of the population that were found to be associated with attitudes, education and race especially, provide an initial direction to the discussion of television's audience, which follows in the next chapter.

CHAPTER 3

TELEVISION'S AUDIENCE

By all available measures, the amount of time the average American spends before his TV set increased during the ten years that separated the two studies. The figures in Table 3-1 from the Nielsen Company's tabulations show the ten-year trend in total household viewing (anyone in the house can be watching).

table 3-1
Amount of Household Viewing (hours per home per day—yearly average)

1960	5 hours 3 minutes
1962	5 hours 6 minutes
1964	5 hours 25 minutes
1966	5 hours 32 minutes
1968	5 hours 46 minutes
1970	5 hours 56 minutes

Source: *Dimensions of Television*, published periodically by the National Association of Broadcasters.

table 3-2

"On an average day, during what hours do you yourself ordinarily watch television?"

(likely viewing 1960–1970)

	PERCENTAGE CHECKING EACH TIME PERIOD					
HOURS	Weekdays		Saturday		Sunday	
	1960	1970	1960	1970	1960	1970
Morning:						
6:00– 7:00	2	4	1	2	1	2
7:00– 8:00	5	8	1	4	1	3
8:00– 9:00	6	8	3	7	2	7
9:00–10:00	8	8	5	8	4	7
10:00–11:00	10	12	6	9	5	8
11:00–12:00	12	15	7	10	6	10
Afternoon:						
12:00– 1:00	14	21	8	14	9	15
1:00– 2:00	12	18	13	17	14	21
2:00– 3:00	13	19	15	21	19	26
3:00– 4:00	11	17	13	21	20	26
4:00– 5:00	11	19	12	20	21	24
Early Evening:						
5:00– 6:00	16	31	14	24	22	25
6:00– 7:00	35	55	29	40	35	39
Evening:						
7:00– 8:00	57	63	50	53	52	56
8:00– 9:00	69	69	57	60	61	65
9:00–10:00	66	66	56	58	58	63
10:00–11:00	42	48	40	46	38	44
Late Evening, Early Morning:						
11:00–12:00	15	20	20	24	14	17
12:00– 1:00	7	7	9	11	6	5
1:00– 2:00	2	3	3	5	2	2
2:00– 3:00	1	2	1	3	1	1

Base: 1960 100 percent = 2427
1970 100 percent = 1900

The Nielsen estimates show an increase in viewing over the ten-year span of about 17 percent. In the Steiner study, and again in 1970, the national sample's viewing was measured by means of a somewhat imprecise technique. About half way through the interview the respondents were given a sheet marked off in boxes for each hour during an average weekday and an average Saturday and Sunday, on which they were asked to check the times when they were "likely to see at least some television." It is a procedure that would tend to produce inflated estimates of viewing: "some television" during the hour could be fifteen minutes worth. The trend that emerges from this method, nevertheless, is very similar to that produced by the more refined methods of the rating services. In 1960, the average number of hours checked per day was 4.1; in 1970 it was 4.9, or an increase of nearly 20 percent. Table 3-2 shows the hours of "likely" viewing for 1960 and 1970 so that the times of day when the audience has increased may be seen.

Most of the increase in viewing would appear to have come during the less attended daytime hours and during the 5:00 to 7:00 evening news period; very little of it in the prime time hours of 7:00 to 11:00. Perhaps, by 1960, the average amount of viewing during the most popular of all times, especially 8:00 to 10:00 P.M., had already approached a practical maximum. Given some people who will refrain from watching under almost any circumstance, some who work in the evening, others whose activities must take them out of the house, and the occasional set in bad repair, it could be that the potential average audience is considerably less than everybody, and there were few after 1960 that could have been added to it.

THE EQUAL-OPPORTUNITY AUDIENCE

As with the gross attitude scores and the shifts in attitude that were discussed previously, we can subject the data on the amount of time people spend watching television to a multivariate analysis. Are there particular types of people who view considerably more than others? Has the composition of the light viewing and the heavy viewing groups changed in the course of ten years? There are, of course, some things already known about the viewing of subgroups from rating services and other data. Women on the average watch considerably more television than men in the course of a week. Both men and women over fifty watch more than young men and women. Lower-income and lower-education groups would appear to watch a bit more than those of a higher socioeconomic status, and the teen-agers appear not to have kept up with their viewing as well as others.

31

Clearly, some of these variations in total amount of viewing may be no more than variations in the available opportunities to watch. The housewife and the older retired man could, conceivably, watch television all day long whereas the working man is limited to evenings and weekends. In the analysis that follows, we have attempted to reduce the effect of such unequal opportunities by restricting the viewing times to be considered to those hours when at least most of the adult population could if they wished, sit in their living rooms with the set turned on—weekdays from 6 P.M. on, and all day Saturday and Sunday.

The results of the AID analyses employing the same variables as were used in the previous analyses of attitude scores, are shown in Charts 3-1 and 3-2.

It is worth noting, first, that there are two factors that do not emerge as significant determinants of viewing in either of the analyses. Sex, the most consistent variable in over-all viewing, plays no part at all in predicting viewing when opportunities are equalized. Education, which makes a large difference in how people feel about television, made no difference at all in 1970 in how much they watched it. In 1960 it appeared in a minor role as an ultimate split of a group of variously aged Republicans and Democrats in five geographic regions (living mainly in large cities) which is a hard-to-interpret finding and suggests a chance variation in the data. In a word, when opportunities are equalized and other characteristics of viewers are taken into account, these two otherwise important characteristics disappear from the equation. Family composition (here defined as the presence or absence of children under 15 in the household) also fails to appear as a factor affecting viewing any more than it did as a factor affecting general attitudes.

The characteristics that do survive the computer's manipulations do not give us a very clear picture of what makes for a heavy or light viewer. In 1960 we find size of place on top of the hierarchy, with heavier viewing in large cities and towns of less than 2500 and lighter viewing in the middle-sized cities and rural areas. Further down, race, geographic region, religion, political preference and age and a few others make some slight difference. But it would probably be a mistake to venture interpretations of the variations produced by these factors. No one of them is more than a very risky predictor of viewing. In fact all eleven variables combined in the analysis account for less than 6 percent of the total variance—which tells us that very little can be explained about viewing by referring to the background characteristics of the viewers.

The twelve variables used in the 1970 analysis do not perform even that well as predictors—combined they account for less than 5 percent of the total variance. Region of the country, age, income, conservatism versus

chart 3-1
1960 Viewing

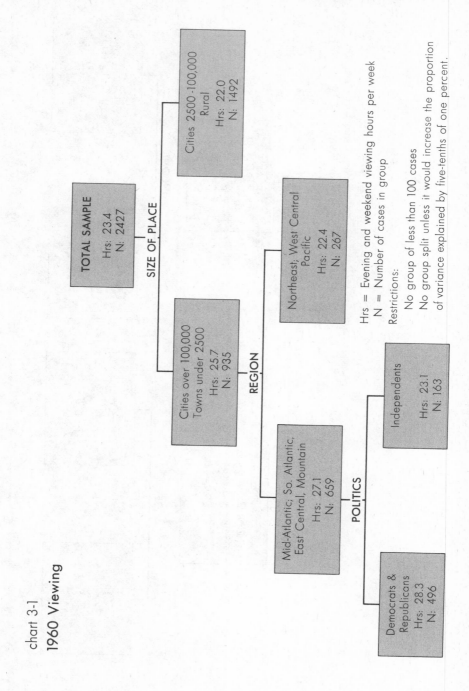

TOTAL SAMPLE
Hrs: 23.4
N: 2427

SIZE OF PLACE

Cities 2500-100,000
Rural
Hrs: 22.0
N: 1492

Cities over 100,000
Towns under 2500
Hrs: 25.7
N: 935

REGION

Northeast; West Central
Pacific
Hrs: 22.4
N: 267

Mid-Atlantic; So. Atlantic,
East Central, Mountain
Hrs: 27.1
N: 659

POLITICS

Independents
Hrs: 23.1
N: 163

Democrats &
Republicans
Hrs: 28.3
N: 496

Hrs = Evening and weekend viewing hours per week
N = Number of cases in group
Restrictions:
  No group of less than 100 cases
  No group split unless it would increase the proportion
  of variance explained by five-tenths of one percent.

chart 3-2
1970 Viewing

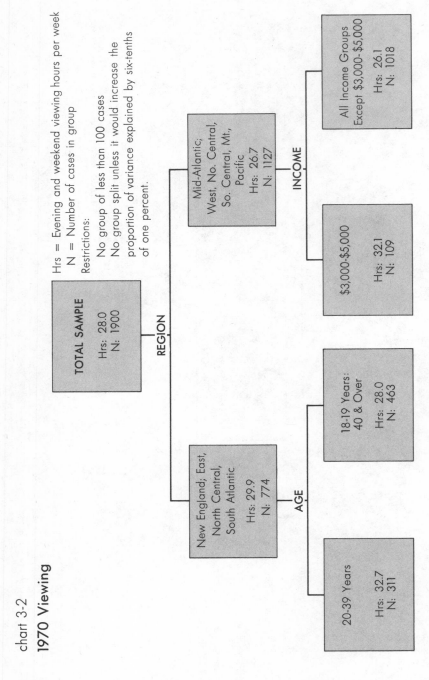

Hrs = Evening and weekend viewing hours per week
N = Number of cases in group
Restrictions:
No group of less than 100 cases
No group split unless it would increase the
proportion of variance explained by six-tenths
of one percent.

TOTAL SAMPLE

Hrs: 28.0
N: 1900

REGION

New England; East,
North Central,
South Atlantic

Hrs: 29.9
N: 774

Mid-Atlantic,
West, No. Central,
So. Central, Mt,
Pacific
Hrs: 26.7
N: 1127

AGE

20-39 Years

Hrs: 32.7
N: 311

18-19 Years:
40 & Over

Hrs: 28.0
N: 463

INCOME

$3,000-$5,000

Hrs: 32.1
N: 109

All Income Groups
Except $3,000-$5,000

Hrs: 26.1
N: 1018

liberalism, and occupation all play some miniscule part in the analysis, in an ambiguous set of interrelationships, but no one of these factors by itself accounts for more than one percent of the explained variance.

The one main conclusion that may be drawn from this analysis is that the amount of time a person will spend watching television during the evening and weekend hours has little to do with who he is as a socially defined entity. Stated another way, the equal opportunity audience of television is an extraordinarily undifferentiated one in its social composition. It would appear to be very much of a "mass" audience if we mean by that term a large audience and one composed of all segments of the population in fairly equal proportions.

THE EDUCATED VIEWER

With the appearance of such data, an anomaly in the findings emerges. It seems that the educated viewer who holds a lower opinion of television than others, grasps the opportunities available to him to watch it just about as much as anyone else. Steiner, a decade earlier, noticed this discrepancy between attitudes and actions among the better educated and at one point attributed it to a tendency toward intellectual conformity among the college educated. The educated man felt (or knew) that his social peers were rather down on television and he, therefore, did not want to breach the peer-group expectation by praising it. Steiner also suggested that higher education produces a sense of proportion in adopting points of view, a predilection for the balanced, moderate position which inhibits the expressions of high enthusiasm or extreme vilification that might otherwise burst forth. Together those two propositions may help to explain the generally lower attitude scores among the better educated and the relatively few "superfans" we find among them, even though they are watching about as much as anyone else.

Rolf Meyersohn, in reanalysing data from the 1960 study, paid considerable attention to the educated viewer and cast some further light on his dilemma.[1] Meyersohn constructed a "discrepancy ratio" for the answers to Steiner's questions—the discrepancy between what an individual thought was the "right" amount of TV viewing and how much he actually watched. The better educated revealed the greater discrepancy —they watched more than they thought they should—while the less educated had a hard time reaching their viewing norms. Meyersohn is able to

---

[1] Rolf Meyersohn. *Leisure and Television: A Study in Compatibility*, Ph.D. Dissertation, Columbia University, 1965.

explain the phenomenon of a high discrepancy ratio in large part as resulting from an orientation to printed matter—to "book culture"—an affliction to which the better educated are peculiarly susceptible and which infects the college man with beliefs about appropriate behavior that he cannot quite live up to, as long as that TV set is around.

The sense of guilt about television viewing, to which the educated viewer would be particularly prone, can be examined rather directly from answers to a question that was included in both surveys. People were asked whether indeed they thought they were watching too little or too much television, with results as shown in Chart 3-3.

The 1960 tendency for the better educated to feel they were

chart 3-3
By Education of Respondent

"Do you think that you spend too much time watching television or would you say that you don't have a chance to see as much as you would really like to see?"

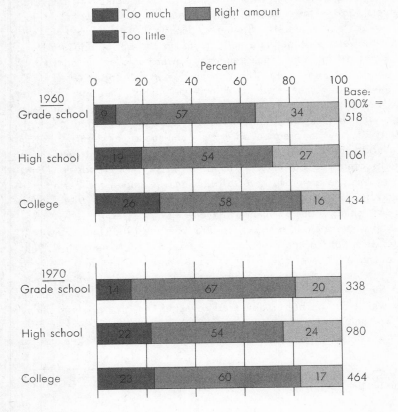

36

watching too much, and the less educated to feel they were watching too little, persists to some extent in 1970. But it is interesting to note that the differences have narrowed. The proportion of the grade school educated watching too much has increased a bit, but the proportion of that group watching too little has decreased. For the college educated, the proportion watching too much has decreased. Is the college-educated viewer finding a way out of his dilemma while the viewer with less education is starting to worry about his excesses? These initial comparisons would suggest such a change in the population. We will return to the question in subsequent chapters.

THE AGES OF VIEWING: GENERATIONS AND LIFE CYCLES

One of the more interesting speculations about television in American society embodies the concept of a TV generation—a generation of viewers whose ideas have been uniquely shaped by television because they grew up with it and received its impact while in their early formative years. An extension of this concept might be called the "generational" theory —the theory that the early adopted ideas persist as people grow older, leading to a gradual change in the society as a whole as new generations grow up and older generations die off. Some political theorists have suggested that long-term trends toward liberalism or conservatism have resulted from the persistence of new ideology within generations while the older ideology is taken to the grave.[2]

An alternative view—the "life cycle" theory—suggests that people do change their views as they grow older. In a few years the teen-agers leave home, get married, and start raising families; young men and some young women start their careers of work; people become more settled in their communities and accumulate possessions; older people become more isolated as the children leave home and as disability impedes their mobility. Each cycle of life brings its demands, opportunities, and limitations to remold the ideas with which the generation started.

To a limited extent we can examine the findings of the two surveys from these two opposing points of view. When we discover changes in attitude or in viewing behavior over ten years among respondents of

---

[2] S. M. Lipset and Everett C. Ladd, Jr., "College Generations from the 1930's to the 1960's," *Public Interest*, Fall 1971, pp. 99–113; William Klecka, "Applying Generations to the Study of Political Behavior. A Cohort Analysis," *Public Opinion Quarterly*, Fall 1971, pp. 358–74; and Cutler Neal, "Generation Maturation and Party Affiliation," *Public Opinion Quarterly*, Winter 1969-1970, pp. 583–589.

various age groups, do they better fit the generational or the life-cycle model? We cannot, of course, trace the changes, or lack of them, for particular individuals, since we are dealing with two independent samples. But we can examine age cohorts—for example, the group of 28- and 29-year-olds in the 1970 sample, who (we hope) are similar in the aggregate to the 18- and 19-year-olds from the 1960 sample—except for the added ten years of life. If we find pronounced changes in the views of such cohorts, then we may cautiously infer that the former teen-agers' views have changed by the time they reached their late twenties. If we find no change by this type of analysis, then we can infer that the attitudes are relatively stable and unaffected by the process of aging for a generation of viewers.

Either or both of these phenomena may appear as components of the several over-all ten-year trends that have been observed so far—the decrease in favorable attitudes toward television, for instance, or the 17 to 20 percent increase in viewing; but it is highly unlikely that any major societal trend in attitudes or behavior could be explained by a generational interpretation when we have only a ten-year period in which to observe the movements of generations. Similarly, the modification of attitudes through aging that is implicit in the life-cycle interpretation should be observed at more points in time before one could adopt it as a viable theory. The best we can do is examine the age-related changes between the two surveys with the two opposing interpretations in mind, testing them against the expectations one would have from the standpoint of each of the theories.

Table 3-3 which shows the proportion choosing television among the products and services "you are most satisfied with," for various age groups in 1960 and 1970, serves both to illustrate a method of cohort comparison and to introduce a first finding. Horizontally we can compare people of the same ages at two points in time; diagonally we observe several age cohorts, in 1960 and a decade later when they are ten years older.

The over-all downward trend in satisfaction with television applies to all the comparisons. The people in their forties in 1970 are less "satisfied" than the 40-year-olds of 1960; and the 1970 40-year-olds are less satisfied than their 30-year-old surrogates of ten years earlier; so the over-all societal trend is there, affecting all the variations. We may still assume, however, that if the changes are relatively small within the cohorts (the diagonal percentage differences) the generational interpretation is supported; people tend to persist in their attitudes over a ten-year span of life. Relatively small differences *between* age groups (the horizontal differences) would support a life-cycle interpretation, with views changing

table 3-3

"With which of these five things are you personally most satisfied (fashions for women, automobiles, television programs, movies, and popular music)?"

PERCENT SAYING TELEVISION PROGRAMS

Age	1960	1970	Base: 100 percent = 1960	1970
18–19	17	10	84	182
20–27	} 28	17	473	261
28–29		13 } 16		70 } 331
30–39	26	11	544	356
40–49	25	12	463	377
50–59	30	16	400	311
60+	43	27	440	419
Total	29	16	2404	1976

graph 1

Percentage of Those Who Reply: "Television"

"With which of these five things are you personally most satisfied?"

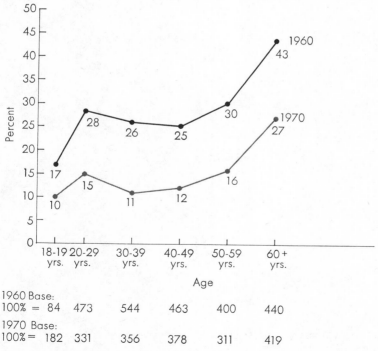

Age

1960 Base:
100% = 84   473   544   463   400   440

1970 Base:
100% = 182   331   356   378   311   419

Mean of horizontal variations, less trend: 2.2
Mean of diagonal variations, less trend: 5.6

as people grow older. One way to measure these relative variations is to compute an average of the horizontal and an average of the diagonal variations, in each case adjusting for the over-all trend figures. We assume for our present purpose that the over-all trend—such as a general decrease in favorable attitudes or an across-the-board increase in viewing—is a phenomenon of society at large, potentially affecting all groups equally, which needs to be taken into account in our calculations. In the case of Table 3-3, the average horizontal variation is relatively small (2.2) and the average diagonal variation relatively large (5.6)—in support of the life-cycle interpretation over the generational.[3]

graph 2

"Here are some things that many people take for granted today. But imagine, if you can, that for two or three months you could have only one of these and have to do without the rest. Which one would you choose?"

Percent Who Chose Television (1st and 2nd choice combined)
By Age

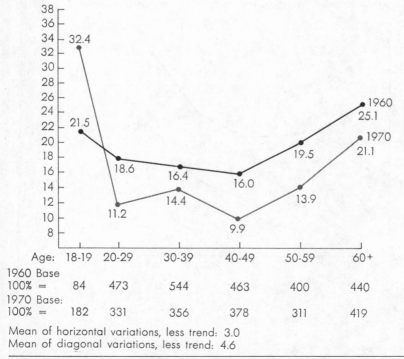

Age:	18-19	20-29	30-39	40-49	50-59	60+
1960 Base 100% =	84	473	544	463	400	440
1970 Base: 100% =	182	331	356	378	311	419

Mean of horizontal variations, less trend: 3.0
Mean of diagonal variations, less trend: 4.6

[3] See Appendix Statistical Note for the derivation of these measures.

This and other 1960–1970 comparisons among age groups can perhaps best be seen by graphs, as on the following pages. In Graph 1, the lines connecting the proportion of people choosing television as the most satisfactory of the five items show almost identical patterns. At each age, there are fewer "most satisfieds" with television in 1970 than in 1960, a reflection of the over-all trend. But the scenario remains the same. TV does not compete well with other items, especially automobiles among the teen-agers; it improves its position among the newly married, but reaches the high point among the old. In the second graph, there is again a similarity between the 1960 and 1970 patterns. In this case, the proportions who would not want to do without television for a few months are high among the young and the old; but television does not compete as well with other things (refrigerators, automobiles, telephones and newspapers) in the in-between years.

Graph 3, on summary attitude scores, also shows the young folk and the old folk sharing similar views—in this case relatively high attitudes toward television, with the middle-aged groups deviating toward a less favorable view. Graph 4 once again shows a curvilinear pattern in 1960 that is rather faithfully repeated in the 1970 population. The proportion of adults who think that children are "better off" with television than they

graph 3

Attitude toward Television

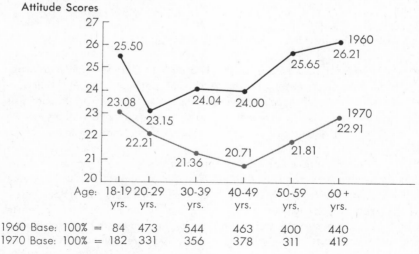

Mean of horizontal variations, less trend: .9
Mean of diagonal variations, less trend: 1.4

graph 4

Percent Who Say "Better off <u>With</u>"

"There has been a lot of discussion about the possible
effects of television on children. Taking everything
into consideration, would you say that children
are better off with or without television?"

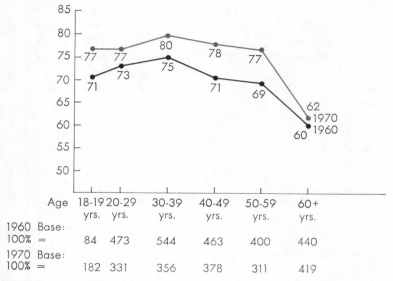

Age	18-19 yrs.	20-29 yrs.	30-39 yrs.	40-49 yrs.	50-59 yrs.	60+ yrs.
1960 Base: 100% =	84	473	544	463	400	440
1970 Base: 100% =	182	331	356	378	311	419

Mean of horizontal variations, less trend: 1.7
Mean of diagonal variations, less trend: 2.2

would be without it, is smaller at the two ends of the life-cycle and larger
in the middle. The reason for this particular pattern is, in all likelihood,
attributable to parenthood. As will be shown in Chapter 7, the benefits
of television to children are seen more by parents than by others, so we
would expect a higher rating on that aspect of the medium in the child-
rearing years.

In all of these graphs the pattern would seem to indicate what the
statistical measures tend to confirm—people change their views about
television as they reach different stages in life. In three out of four cases,
things happening early and things happening late in life seem to produce
favorable attitudes and something else in the middle years tends to depress
the attitudes a bit. In the other case the curves are reversed but with an
explanation for their shape—the presence or absence of children—that fits
a life-cycle interpretation.

graph 5

Amount of Viewing

Amount of Viewing Scores *

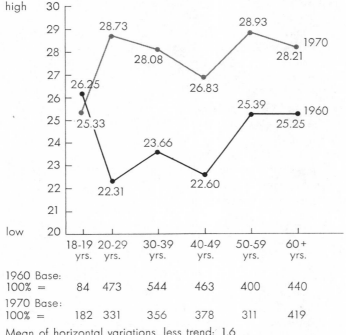

1960 Base:
100% =   84   473   544   463   400   440

1970 Base:
100% =   182   331   356   378   311   419

Mean of horizontal variations, less trend: 1.6
Mean of diagonal variations, less trend: 1.9

*Number of hours viewed per week: evenings and weekend.

It is, of course, not necessary to assume that the relatively high regard for television shared by the very young and the old stems from the same reasons. On the contrary we would speculate, without much data to inhibit the speculation, that television serves quite different functions for the two age groups. The teen-agers in our sample, and in the 1960 sample, are relatively well educated. They have grown up with television, most of them, as a normal, accepted everyday piece of household equipment like the refrigerator in the kitchen or the car in the garage. It is unlikely that TV has for them the mystique of innovation, but we can imagine it is regarded with the unthinking affection that one has for the very familiar—without it life would seem abnormal. Many older viewers are less educated and thus share with others of lower socioeconomic status a generally fa-

43

vorable view of the medium that provides them with the entertainment and information they find more difficult to get elsewhere. They are also more apt to be dependent on television because of restricted mobility and solitude. The old and the young, in any case, hold very different views about some of the *content* of television, as we will see later; what they share is a high regard at a very general attitudinal level.

We come finally to the very pronounced changes in the age patterns found in the last of the five graphs—on the amount of television viewing. In 1960, the heaviest viewing was found among teen-agers. In 1970, teen-agers watched less than any of the other age groups. In absolute terms the decline in teen-age viewing was small, but if we were to take the 1960 distribution of viewing by age groups as the norm and then add the over-all ten-year increase in viewing, the relative decline among teen-agers becomes huge. For the two groups of 20–28 year-olds, also, the amount of viewing diverges—rather low in 1960 relative to the other ages and rather high in 1970. Only after 30 do the two lines parallel one another in a pattern that we would associate with the life-cycle interpretation. These changes may be seen more precisely in Table 3-4.

table 3-4
Median Hours of Viewing per Week (1960 and 1970)

Age	1960	1970	Base: 100 percent = 1960	1970	
18–19	26.25	25.33	84	182	
20–27	} 22.31	29.05 } 28.70	473	261 } 331	
28–29		27.33		70	
30–39	23.66	28.08	544	356	
40–49	22.60	26.83	463	378	
50–59	25.39	28.93	400	311	
60+	25.25	28.21	440	419	
Total	23.82	28.20	2404	1977	

All the 1960 age cohorts did increase their viewing by the time they became ten years older, with the increase for the 18- and 19-year-old cohort less than for others. Perhaps, for the 1960 teen-agers viewing was for some reasons peculiarly high and they couldn't keep pace with the rest in *increasing* their amount of viewing. And it may be that there is something of a transitory nature in the life-cycle of the new 1970 crop of teen-agers that has depressed their viewing rates. If it is a phase they are just

passing through, we might expect an adjustment in the future to the viewing hours of the older age groups. But if it happens to be a way of life
that will endure as the generation ages—the generational hypothesis—
the days of the upward trend in television viewing are numbered.

THE NEGRO AUDIENCE

We saw in the previous chapter that in 1970 race was the best predictor
of people's general attitude toward television, better than age, education,
sex, or any of eight other characteristics. The average attitude score
among blacks is 28, out of a maximum of 35; among whites it is 22.

The difference between the two groups is more dramatically shown
by the proportion of superfans to be found among them—those enthusiasts
who select the extremely favorable positions in the battery of adjectives
that make up the attitude scale. The proportions of extremists on ten items
are shown in Table 3-5.

Clearly, the black segment of the sample contains a much higher
proportion of enthusiasts than the white—perhaps half of them could be
classified as superfans.

With that finding to ponder, we can proceed to a further account

table 3-5
Percent of Viewers Taking the Most Favorable Position on a Six-Point Scale

Television is:	RACE	
	White	Black
Exciting	15	58
In Good Taste	14	56
Important	26	65
Excellent	12	43
Relaxing	29	62
Interesting	28	61
Wonderful	14	58
For Me	24	58
Getting Better	12	46
Informative	32	61
Base: 100 percent =	(1710)	(190)

of the characteristics and attitudes of the Negro audience—but not before a cautionary remark or two. Any small segment of the total sample, in this case a total of 194 blacks, has a good chance of misrepresenting its parameter population, in this case all blacks over 17 in the United States in 1970. On some characteristics the black sample diverges from the U. S. Census figures. Forty-seven percent of U. S. adult Negroes are men, 51 percent in the sample. The sample's educational and age distributions are close to the census figures, but we did end up with too many *older males* (over 50) and too few young ones (20-29), and among the females there are too few very young (18-19) and old (over 60) and somewhat too many in the intervening ages. Such vagaries of sampling could throw the results off a bit, to the extent that these characteristics are related to attitudes, but it is unlikely that the sampling errors could explain entirely the very pronounced black-white differences that we find.

The black audience's high general regard for television is reflected in its views about various aspects of television content. The blacks are considerably less critical, for instance, of TV commercials. Only 49 percent think there are "too many"—74 percent for whites; 84 percent find TV commercials "helpful," 53 percent among the whites; 28 percent of the blacks and 51 percent of the whites "would prefer TV without any commercials." On questions about television news, we find that the black viewer is less apt to think that newscasters "bias" the news; more of them gave television an "excellent" rating in its coverage of the 1968 presidential campaign, and more of them feel that television helped them decide on their candidate. Blacks also see more improvement in television than is perceived by the white audience. And black parents see a more benign effect of television on their children—the child who "sees a lot of television" is apt to have the advantage over the child who sees very little, in the view of more of the black parents.

Throughout the interviews, whenever the questions called for rather direct expressions of attitudes, the black audience appeared to be more favorable toward television. But as we get closer to behavior, as reported by the respondents, this rather consistent picture becomes a bit blurred. We would expect, if all were to hang together properly, that blacks would watch more television since favorable attitudes and amount of viewing are at least slightly correlated among the population as a whole. As it turns out the black audience in our sample reports an average of 25 hours and 22 minutes of evening and weekend viewing per week, while the white sample reports 28 hours and 23 minutes.[4] Tabulated below are the results

---

[4] Bogart reports a slightly higher amount of viewing for blacks than for whites when total weekly viewing is taken into account. Bogart, *The Age of Television*, p. 377.

of three questions (Tables 3-6, 3-7, and 3-8) related to the amount of viewing:

table 3-6
Amount of Viewing by Race

	White	Black
Heavy Viewers (35 or more hours)	33	37
Average Viewers (21–34 hours)	36	19
Light Viewers (Up to 20 hours per week) ..	30	44
Base: 100 percent = ...	(1665)	(190)

Taking these three items together, we find the black audience with a higher proportion of light TV viewers, but with more of them feeling that their viewing has been on the increase and with double the proportion feeling that they do not watch as much as they would like—the picture of a well-disposed audience on the increase.

Could this all be the result of less education in the black population? We know that the less educated tend to like television better, and that blacks, by and large, are less educated than whites. In our sample 35 percent of the blacks have never reached high school (17 percent of the whites). Among the whites, 28 percent have had at least a year of college —13 percent of the blacks. Education, as an important predictor of atti-

table 3-7
"Do you find that you yourself are now watching TV more, or less, or about the same as you were ten years ago?"
(responses of those 28 years or older)

	VIEWING MORE/LESS	
	White	Black
More	38	53
Same	31	29
Less	31	18
Base: 100 percent = ...	(1315)	(133)

table 3-8

"Do you think that you spend too much time watching television, or that you don't see as much as you would really like to see?"

	White	Black
Too Little	19	38
Right Amount	58	49
Too Much	21	11
Base: 100 percent = ...	(1601)	(180)

tudes toward television might be expected to account for the observed differences; but apparently it does not (Table 3-9).

At each educational level, television receives a better rating among blacks than among whites, as may be seen by the average attitude scores at the bottom of the columns. Among both groups, the proportion of people with very favorable attitudes falls as education increases—but much more sharply among the whites than among the blacks. The proportion with low scores increases with education among the whites, but actually decreases among blacks. The college-educated white has a medium to *low* regard for television, the college-educated black a medium to *high* regard, if we may judge from the rather small number of cases in the sample. It appears that among blacks the usual, oft-noted, relationship between education and attitudes does not obtain.

In other respects as well, education seems to have a different impact on the black audience (Tables 3-10, 3-11, and 3-12).

table 3-9

Attitude toward Television by Race and Education of Respondents (expressed in percentages)

	Grade School		High School		College	
ATTITUDE	White	Black	White	Black	White	Black
High	38	68	27	60	14	56
Medium	41	18	46	29	45	40
Low	22	14	27	11	41	4
Base: 100 percent = .	(287)	(66)	(912)	(99)	(459)	(24)
Average Attitude Score.	24	28	22	28	19	27

table 3-10
Amount of Viewing (proportion of "heavy" viewers)

	Percent			
EDUCATION	White (Base)		Black (Base)	
Grade School	40	(287)	29	(66)
High School	33	(912)	39	(99)
College	29	(459)	48	(24)
TOTAL	33	(1658)	37	(189)

table 3-11
Watching More, Less, About the Same as Ten Years Ago: Proportion Saying "More" (responses of those 28 years or older)

	Percent			
EDUCATION	White Percent (Base)		Black Percent (Base)	
Grade School	48	(271)	57	(53)
High School	37	(711)	48	(65)
College	31	(333)	60	(15)
TOTAL	38	(1315)	53	(133)

table 3-12
Watching too Much, too Little or the Right Amount? Proportion Saying "too Little"

	Percent			
EDUCATION	White Percent (Base)		Black Percent (Base)	
Grade School	16	(287)	27	(65)
High School	21	(912)	41	(98)
College	14	(459)	40	(25)
TOTAL	18	(1658)	38	(188)

In the population at large, the proportion of "heavy" viewers, those who report they are likely to watch some television more than 35 hours per week during evenings and weekends, declines with education; in the black audience the proportion of heavy viewers is higher among the better educated. Similarly, the college-educated blacks are most apt to report that they have increased their viewing; among the whites it is the grade school viewers more than others who say that their viewing has increased. And the better-educated blacks, more than the less-educated, feel they are watching too little. The data clearly do not support the image of a black TV fan that associates him with the less-educated white viewer, because that is where his general educational level places him in the American hierarchy.

Leo Bogart, in analyzing a much larger sample of black viewers, also discovered that the blacks did not vary in their amount of viewing by socioeconomic status in the same manner as the whites. The higher income and higher-educated blacks watched more than other blacks, a finding that Bogart attributes to TV viewing by upper-income black women.[5] If education has any effect at all on the viewing and attitudes of the black population, it is not the same effect it has on whites. It does not act as a restriction on viewing, nor is it a restraining force on the expression of favorable attitudes as it is for the white majority. If anything, the effects are the opposite.

THE AUDIENCE OF EDUCATIONAL TELEVISION

In 1960, there were 44 public television stations broadcasting throughout the United States. By 1970, this segment of the television industry had grown to 184 stations with an estimated audience of 24 million viewers per week. While typically referred to as "educational television" (the term we used in this survey) specific educational or instructional content is only one, although a substantial, aspect of its programming. Serious drama, documentaries and news analyses, public-service programs and informative children's shows, as well as some rather innovative presentations considered too controversial for commercial television, are some of the types of broadcasts which have found their way into public television.

Because its major expansion and public acceptance only occurred after the 1960 survey, the subject of public television was only faintly touched then and the very small number of ETV viewers did not warrant

---

[5] Leo Bogart, "Negro and White Media Exposure: New Evidence," *Journalism Quarterly*, Spring 1972, pp. 15–21.

any discussion in Steiner's report. While the 1970 statistics do not point to any very dramatic invasion of ETV into commercial television's audience, they do indicate a growing awareness of the noncommercial medium. The 1970 survey reveals that 50 percent of the respondents in all television households were aware of being able to receive an educational station, and that 96 percent of this group could identify the station channel by number. While this 50 percent may be an underestimate of the actual availability of ETV to the public, there are numerous restrictions on reception which should be pointed out. One of the most obviously important is that an individual must live in an area where ETV signals penetrate. In 1970 there were three states (Alaska, Wyoming, and Montana) with no public television stations at all, and there are vast areas of the west and midwest where terrain or distance from stations also precludes viewing for portions of the population. Given these limitations, it has been estimated that between 71 and 76 percent of the total U.S. population reside in areas where ETV might be received. Another limitation is that 106 out of the 184 ETV stations operating in 1970 transmitted on the UHF band. Since UHF receivers were not required on new television sets until after 1964, those with older sets, or 37 percent of the television households, could not receive broadcasts transmitted on UHF. And even for the sets equipped with UHF loop antennas, some ETV signals may be of too poor a quality for the householder to believe he is "receiving" it.

With these limitations it is quite possible that only about half the viewers could receive ETV programs with what they considered tolerable clarity in 1970. Other estimates are higher. Louis Harris and Associates concluded that about 57 percent of the 1970 U.S. households could receive either a VHF or UHF educational station.[6] Our somewhat lower estimate may exclude a number of people who were able to receive a clear picture on the ETV channel but were unaware of that fact.

The distribution of properly equipped sets, in places where ETV is available, definitely favors the more affluent and better educated viewer. Our survey found only 27 percent of the population with grade school education able to receive an educational station, compared to 63 percent among the college educated (Table 3-13). Other studies have shown a similar, and associated discrepancy between the poorer and the wealthier viewers, the latter having the distinct advantage.

The reports of our respondents on their actual viewing of ETV help further to define an audience already limited by the restrictions on availa-

---

[6] Louis Harris and Associates, Inc., *The Viewing of Public Television* prepared for The Corporation for Public Broadcasting, 1970.

table 3-13
Percent Able to Receive an ETV Channel

		Base: 100% =
Grade School	27	(345)
High School	51	(1011)
College	63	(480)

bility. Chart 3-4 is based upon responses of the half-sample who say they can receive an ETV station on their sets. It shows the proportions of various subgroups saying that they watch it at all and the proportions of more serious viewers—those who report watching at least once a week.

The series of questions used in the survey produces a total proportion of 66 percent of those who receive ETV saying that they watch it at all; and 40 percent saying that they watch it as often as once a week (Chart 3-4). The comparable figures for the whole U.S. population would be 33 percent and 20 percent, respectively.

Among the subgroups, the difference between the less and better educated is again pronounced. Among those grade school graduates who can receive ETV, only 53 percent watch at all and 24 percent watch once a week or more. Among those with some college the comparable percentages are 78 and 51 percent. Again if we were to translate the viewing proportions of the three educational groups back to the total population (receivers and nonreceivers combined) we would have the following estimates (Table 3-14).

table 3-14
Percent Watching ETV: Total Sample, by Education

	PERCENT WATCHING AT ALL	PERCENT WATCHING AT LEAST ONCE A WEEK	Base: 100% =
Grade School	14	6	345
High School	32	18	1011
College	48	33	480
Total	33	20	1836

chart 3-4
Viewing of Educational Television
(by those who can receive it)

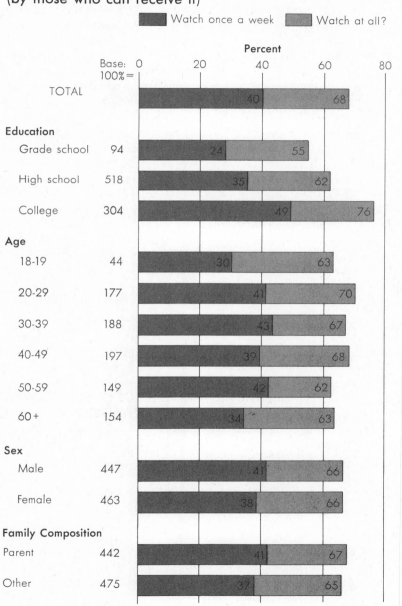

█ Watch once a week   ▓ Watch at all?

Percent

	Base: 100% =	40	68
TOTAL		40	68
Education			
Grade school	94	24	55
High school	518	35	62
College	304	49	76
Age			
18-19	44	30	63
20-29	177	41	70
30-39	188	43	67
40-49	197	39	68
50-59	149	42	62
60+	154	34	63
Sex			
Male	447	41	66
Female	463	38	66
Family Composition			
Parent	442	41	67
Other	475	37	65

This concentration of educational television viewing among the better educated may be one exception to the general finding (mentioned above and discussed in more detail later) of a surprising similarity among all educational groups in television viewing habits. But it should be noted that even though the college educated watch ETV considerably more than the less educated, the total time they spend in that pursuit is still small. Estimating from our data, the median amount of weekly viewing of the college educated, among those who watch ETV at all, is one hour and 50 minutes, and only 14 percent of that group (about 6 percent of *all* college-educated) report watching as much as five hours a week. ETV has not yet seriously altered the over-all viewing patterns even of the college educated.

Among the age groups, the young and old—under 20 and over 60—share in a relative lack of attention to educational television. The viewers are found more frequently in the in-between years when there are more apt to be children around the house. That in turn is related to the last two bars in Chart 3-4, which shows a difference between parents with children under 15 and all others; having a child around would appear to increase the likelihood of watching ETV to some slight extent.

We tried a second-hand assessment of children's viewing of educational television by asking everybody in the sample who could receive it whether anyone else in the house watched as much as once a week. Parents could have reported on their spouses or on other adults who happened to be around, but most reports concerned children under 15 (Table 3-15).

table 3-15

"Do you watch educational television once a week or more often? Who else in the family watches television as often as once a week?"

MENTIONS BY PARENTS OF OTHER'S VIEWING IN PERCENTAGES

No one else watches	35
Children under 15 mentioned	58
Other adults mentioned	25

Base: 100 percent = 440
The question permits multiple mentions.

These reports by parents of their children's viewing depend rather heavily on ages of the children who happen to be around the house. The older the children the less likely they are to be reported as once-a-week viewers, as we can see on Chart 3-5.

The viewing reported by the age of children would indicate a

chart 3-5

Parents' Reports of Children's Viewing
(by ages of children under 15)

"Do any other members of your family watch educational television once a week or more often?"

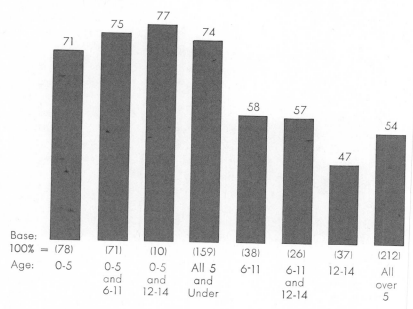

Base: 100% =	(78)	(71)	(10)	(159)	(38)	(26)	(37)	(212)
Age:	0-5	0-5 and 6-11	0-5 and 12-14	All 5 and Under	6-11	6-11 and 12-14	12-14	All over 5

rather substantial toddler's audience of educational television. It is not surprising that *Sesame Street* far outnumbers all other programs mentioned when we asked our sample what programs they remember having seen on ETV recently—though one suspects that recall of that particular program was aided by the publicity it has received.

Though the adult audience of ETV is weighted toward parents, and though a substantial toddler's audience seems to be viewing (and, one might presume, influencing the viewing of the elders), our data do not quite justify a *Sesame Street* syndrome label for the ETV audience. Even among parents, there are a substantial number (43 percent of the viewers) who claim that they watch themselves and still fail to report as much as once a week viewing among their children. One *can* safely describe the 1970 adult audience of educational television as composed largely of the well educated, in their middle years, living in the less isolated parts of the country, with an added chance of viewing if a young child is in the house. And to their numbers are added a substantial but unmeasured group of toddlers.

THE SELECTIVE VIEWER

A variety of aids are available to the average viewer who wishes to select a program to watch before he turns on the set. He may consult the listing in his daily newspaper, he may have saved a weekly guide to programs, or he may have noted the advertisements that appear in the press or between programs on television. Or he may simply remember when his favorite programs are on the air. In the 1970 survey we asked one brief series of questions about the frequency with which various means of program selection are used. The results are shown in Chart 3-6.

It would appear that the vast majority "often" needs no more than a good TV memory to make its program selections. For almost everybody (all but 5 percent) *some* program selections can be made without recourse to any external aids. This is not, perhaps, a surprising finding; one might expect no less of an audience that watches television many hours a day, day after day. It does seem to show the extent to which viewing may have become habitual, oriented toward the familiar rather than toward the new and different, and in that sense essentially conservative.

That is not to say that the audience entirely neglects the other means of arriving at a selection. As the chart indicates, most of the viewers often find themselves referring to the weekly guides, either as a jog to memory or as assistance when in search of something new. A large number (35 percent of the total sample, 40 percent of the parents) say that they often leave the selection to other family members. Smaller numbers use the daily listings or explore the channels by twisting the dial. So a variety of mechanisms are in use for deciding on which program to watch; but the impression remains that a great deal of planning in advance is not thought to be necessary by the average viewer. Nineteen percent of the audience does claim often to "look up shows several days in advance," but many more—55 percent of the total—say that they practically never perform that exercise.

The answers to six of the ten items can serve as a rough index of planned viewing, through which we may attempt to identify the planners in the population at large. People who refer to TV guides or daily listings, who look up shows in advance or who select from ads (items 2, 4, 6, and 7) are probably engaged in a more deliberate preselection of their programs than those who do not. On the other hand, the dial twisters or those who just leave the set on (items 5 and 8) are confessing to an unplanned method of selection. The index was formed by giving a weight of *two* to an "often" answer to each of the first four items, an "occasionally" answer received *one*, and "practically never," *zero*. The answers to items 5 and 8 were scored in reverse. This permitted a maximum score of 12 for the high-planner and a minimum score of zero for the very casual selector of pro-

chart 3-6

"Now, would you please tell me something about what you do to decide on which TV programs to watch? For example, do you often, occasionally, or practically never:

■ Often   ▨ Occasionally   ▢ Practically Never

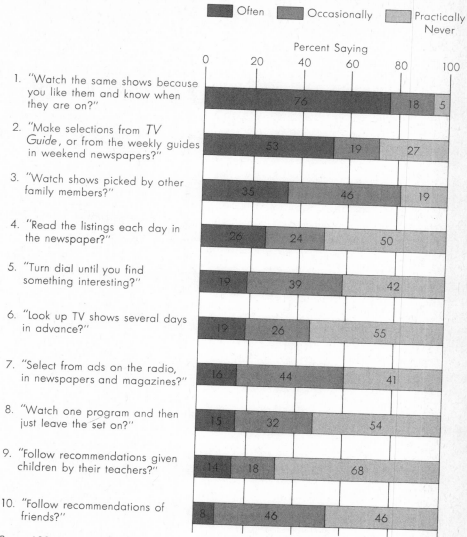

Percent Saying

1. "Watch the same shows because you like them and know when they are on?" — 76 | 18 | 5

2. "Make selections from *TV Guide*, or from the weekly guides in weekend newspapers?" — 53 | 19 | 27

3. "Watch shows picked by other family members?" — 35 | 46 | 19

4. "Read the listings each day in the newspaper?" — 26 | 24 | 50

5. "Turn dial until you find something interesting?" — 19 | 39 | 42

6. "Look up TV shows several days in advance?" — 19 | 26 | 55

7. "Select from ads on the radio, in newspapers and magazines?" — 16 | 44 | 41

8. "Watch one program and then just leave the set on?" — 15 | 32 | 54

9. "Follow recommendations given children by their teachers?" — 14 | 18 | 68

10. "Follow recommendations of friends?" — 8 | 46 | 46

Base: 100 percent = 1900, less no answers, which vary from item to item. The 10 items were presented to the respondents in a different order.

grams. The average score for the population at large turned out to be 6.0.

These scores were submitted to the multivariate analysis of the AID program, again using twelve predictor variables. The results are shown in the next chart.

Three predictors of planned viewing survive the statistical tests used in the analysis. When the interrelationships of the variables are taken into account, a higher degree of planning is found among the better educated—particularly those with at least a high school diploma. The city dweller plans more than those living in towns and rural places, and women more than men, at least in the less-populous areas (Chart 3-7).

The less-educated viewer probably scores low on the planning scale, in part, because he relies less than do others on the printed media for information about most things—including television programs. As a substitute he uses his memory about the programs he likes and then, to a greater extent than others, leaves the initiative to the station to which he is tuned. The proportion of three educational groups who answer "often" to three of the items is instructive on these points (Table 3-16).

table 3-16
Proportion Saying They Often:

ITEM	EDUCATION		
	College	High School	Grade School
Watch the same shows because they like them and know when they are on*	70	78	80
Watch one program and then just leave the set turned to the same station	7	15	24
Make selections from *TV Guide*, or the weekly guides in weekend newspapers	58	57	36
Base: 100 percent = ...	479	1017	348

* Note: This item is not part of the planned-viewing index.

To a moderate extent, some degree of education would appear to make the difference between the viewer of habit and casual chance encounters, and the more deliberate seeker of the choice programs. The educated viewer is more likely to make selections from TV guides; the grade school viewer is more apt to know when his favorite shows are on, or to just leave the set tuned to one channel.

The two other variables appearing in the AID analysis require some comment. The fact that viewers living in more populous places pay attention to the planning of their viewing is hardly surprising. Larger places are apt to have more broadcasting stations, more channels to

chart 3-7
1970 Planned Viewing

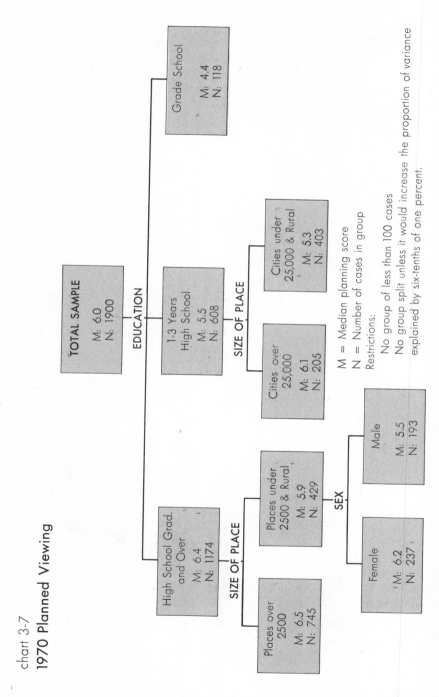

TOTAL SAMPLE
M: 6.0
N: 1900

EDUCATION

High School Grad. and Over
M: 6.4
N: 1174

1-3 Years High School
M: 5.5
N: 608

Grade School
M: 4.4
N: 118

SIZE OF PLACE

Places over 2500
M: 6.5
N: 745

Places under 2500 & Rural
M: 5.9
N: 429

SIZE OF PLACE

Cities over 25,000
M: 6.1
N: 205

Cities under 25,000 & Rural
M: 5.3
N: 403

SEX

Male
M: 5.5
N: 193

Female
M: 6.2
N: 237

M = Median planning score
N = Number of cases in group
Restrictions:
No group of less than 100 cases
No group split unless it would increase the proportion of variance
explained by six-tenths of one percent.

watch and more choices to be made. Cable TV may change all that, eventually, but for the present the isolated viewer has little need for guides and advance notices, or indeed to plan much in advance when the choices are sharply limited.

The higher planning score for women, on the other hand, probably results mainly from the larger amount of time women are apt to spend watching television (if we count their daytime hours along with their "equal opportunity" viewing), and from the greater attention they are able to give to what is written and said about it. The AID results tell us that women plan viewing more than men, even with educational level controlled, but a slight extension of that analysis reveals that the sex differences are not uniform at all educational levels (Chart 3-8).

Among those with high school and college education, a significantly larger proportion of women are high scorers on planning. Among the grade school educated, the difference almost disappears, despite the fact that

chart 3-8
Proportion of High Planners (Scores 8-12)
(by education and sex of respondent)

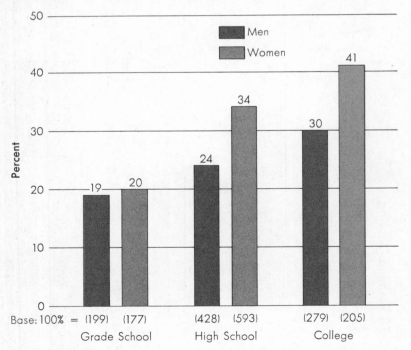

grade school women as well as the better educated ones watch more television than their male counterparts. It would appear that the housewife (the bulk of the female sample is composed of nonworking women) only starts to use the extra time at home in reading about, and planning for, television viewing after a modicum of education beyond the grade school level.

WHY PEOPLE WATCH TELEVISION

The most interesting questions and the most difficult to treat, in a study of this sort, are those of causation. Why do people watch as much television as they do? Why do they select one program rather than another? Why do they hold favorable or critical attitudes toward the medium and what causes them to change their views? The fact that this work, like Steiner's before it, intends to be mainly descriptive of behavior and attitudes, does not quite permit us to avoid an occasional attempt at partial explanation. Education has something to do with the shaping of attitudes toward television. Race, along with education, appears to affect both viewing and views about television. The changes in life style involved in aging would seem to influence some perceptions of the medium. Steiner at one point in his inquiry marched directly into the "causes" of viewing by asking people why they thought they watched, and we followed his lead. Chart 3-9 shows the responses of the 1960 and 1970 populations to a list of fifteen reasons, rearranged according to frequency of choice.

The distributions of reasons in the two surveys are remarkably similar. People are still saying that they watch for the perfectly acceptable reasons of general enjoyment, and to see particular programs, and (somewhat less) to "learn something." They are still eschewing, as personal motivations, the desire for background noise, a fear of missing something, an escape from other activities, and reasons of pure sociability. Perhaps the latter "reasons" seem less legitimate and harder to admit. Steiner notes that his respondents were more apt to ascribe these less-popular reasons to *other* people than to themselves—a projection upon others, he suggests, of motives felt but not accepted for oneself.

Among the minor changes that did occur over the ten-year span, we find that fewer people now than before watch "because it's a pleasant way to spend an evening." Why that is the case is a mystery, but it does seem to have a sex-linked association with the decline in high enthusiasm for television noted in the last chapter. Both sexes provided equal proportions of the superfans of yesteryear, but by 1970 more men had

61

chart 3-9

"Now let's talk for a moment about reasons for watching television. Here is a list of possible reasons. When you watch TV, how often does each of these reasons apply?"

Usually	Occasionally	Rarely	Never

Reason	Year	Usually	Occasionally	Rarely	Never
"To see specific program I enjoy very much."	1960	80		15	2 3
	1970	81		14	3 2
"Because it's a pleasant way to spend an evening."	1960	55	26	11	8
	1970	41	33	16	10
"To see a special program I've heard a lot about."	1960	54	35	7	4
	1970	50	39	8	3
"Because I feel like watching television."	1960	50	23	14	13
	1970	46	29	13	12
"Because I think I can learn something."	1960	36	39	16	9
	1970	34	40	16	10
"Because my husband or wife is or seems to be interested."	1960	21	42	15	22
	1970	20	37	18	25
"Because there is nothing else to do at the time."	1960	20	27	24	29
	1970	27	30	25	19
"Turn on the set to keep me company when I'm alone."	1960	20	25	20	35
	1970	24	23	22	31
"To get away from the ordinary cares and problems of the day."	1960	18	24	25	33
	1970	21	27	25	28
"Mainly to be sociable when others are watching."	1960	17	32	27	24
	1970	15	29	30	26
"Start on one show and then get stuck for the rest of the evening."	1960	15	20	29	36
	1970	14	28	29	30
"Because I'm afraid I might be missing something good."	1960	12	23	28	37
	1970	17	23	32	29
"Because everyone I know is and I want to be able to talk about it afterwards."	1960	8	17	27	48
	1970	9	16	30	45
"Just for background while I'm doing something else."	1960	7	19	25	49
	1970	10	25	25	40
"Keep watching to put off something else I should do."	1960	2	12	27	59
	1970	6	13	28	53

Percentages exclude NA which varies from item to item
1960 Base varies from 1158-1183
1970 Base varies from 1806-1857

dropped out of that category while women better maintained their high allegiance. A similar pattern emerges with the "pleasant evening" reason for viewing, as may be seen in Chart 3-10.

Though men and women tend to share rather similar over-all views toward television, there are a few hints here and there in the 1970 data such as this one—of a slightly less friendly feeling expressed by men.

chart 3-10

Proportions Considering TV "for Me" and "a Pleasant Way to Spend the Evening"

(a)

"When you watch TV, how often does each of these responses apply?"

Percent saying television is: ."For me" (extreme position)

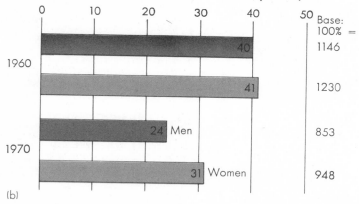

	Base: 100% =
1960	40 → 1146
	41 → 1230
1970	24 Men → 853
	31 Women → 948

(b)

Percent who say they "usually" watch just because "it's such a pleasant way to spend the evening."

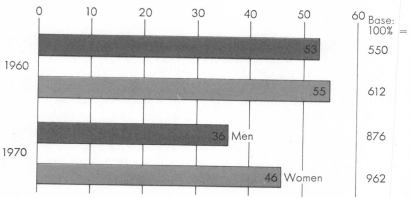

	Base: 100% =
1960	53 → 550
	55 → 612
1970	36 Men → 876
	46 Women → 962

A few of the "less acceptable" reasons on the list are adopted by more of the 1970 than of the 1960 sample. Viewing because "there's nothing else to do," "to put off something else," for "background," and for "company" while alone show slight increases. Although these latter shifts are hardly of major magnitude, they are interesting because they run counter to demographic trends. Each of these reasons is negatively correlated with education—the educated viewer is less likely than others to subscribe to them. With a better-educated population in 1970, we would have expected a decrease where the increases occurred, if nothing else had changed. But, people have changed, if only slightly, toward an increased acceptance of some ancillary psychological functions of television—as a filler of gaps and background voids, as a companion, and as a means of escape from duty.

There is another reason for viewing which the less educated tend to accept more than the better educated—watching "because I think I can learn something." The 1970 answers of three educational groups are shown in Table 3-17. (The 1960 answers were almost identical in distribution.)

table 3-17
Proportion Saying They "Usually" Watch Because They Can Learn Something:

		Base: 100 percent =
Grade School	47	(344)
High School	34	(1008)
College	29	(475)

As we saw a few pages back, the educated viewer is more apt to watch ETV (though even for him, the viewing time is slight); and as will be shown later, the educated viewer is the one who wants more educational material on television. He does not, however, very frequently feel that he is watching because he might learn something. It is quite likely, indeed, that he views most of the television fare he is watching strictly as entertainment. To summarize this composite college-man's views—he doesn't see television as much of a learning experience, but he would like television to be more educational. The composite grade school graduate, on the other hand, sees education—learning something—as a fairly strong motive for watching whatever he watches.

SOME REASONS FOR NOT VIEWING

The interviewing among the subsample of viewers in Minneapolis–St. Paul, 344 cases in all, provided a modest opportunity to explore the obverse to the question "why people watch." What do they do instead? Are there other activities that forcefully compete with America's favorite leisure-time pursuit? During the course of the interview people were asked if they had watched television during the evening before the interview, and then, if they had not, what they had been doing instead (Table 3-18).

table 3-18
"Did you watch any television yesterday evening—anytime after 6 PM? What were you doing instead of watching TV last night?"

	Percent
Yes, viewing television	65
No, outside the home—working	6
No, outside the home—shopping, visiting, out for dinner, church, etc.	16
No, doing chores inside the house (painting, cleaning, etc.)	4
No, other relaxing activity in the home (listening to radio, hi-fi, reading, hobbies, etc.)	8
No, other reasons, NA	1
Base: 100 percent = 344	

There were so many people who had been watching television at some point in the previous evening that we are left with relatively few—about a third of the sample—whose alternative activities could be examined and classified. It is impossible to tell exactly which of these had a fair and realistic choice between television and some other leisure-time activity and chose the latter. But we can safely eliminate as potential viewers those at work; and probably most of the others who were not at home, if we assume that their intramural activities represented necessities ("shopping") or involved prior commitments ("dinner at our friend's home"); and, if those household chores in the next category had to be done last night, we are left with only 8 or 9 percent who had the opportunity but rejected television in favor of some other domestic leisure-time pursuit for a whole evening. These assumptions are too tenuous to permit the assertion that 92 percent of the people in Minneapolis–St. Paul watch television in the evening unless they have something else they *must* do, but the data suggest, at least, that there is not much going on at home for most people that can vie with the attractions of the TV set all evening long. We found a few readers, a few music lovers, and even a few who said they "just sat around" instead of watching television, but it still adds up to a very small group who were not busy and still deliberately chose to do something else for their relaxation or edification.

Having things to do outside the house would appear to be a deterrent to television viewing for more people than attractions at home, even in the late winter and early spring when the interviews were conducted in Minneapolis–St. Paul. At least that was true for our small group of people who did not watch television "last night." To test the proposition in another fashion, we inquired about the sample's nocturnal and other leisure-time activities in general, to see their effect on viewing habits. Do people who generally go out more in the evening usually watch television less? To find out, we asked the question "On the average, about how many times during the seven days in the week do you go out for the evening?" Since we knew from their diaries they had previously kept how long they had spent viewing television during a full week we can relate the two data (Table 3-19).

table 3-19
Frequency of Evening Excursions by Amount of Viewing

	LIGHT VIEWERS (Less than 10 hrs.)	AVERAGE VIEWERS (10-20 hrs.)	HEAVY VIEWERS (More than 20 hrs.)
Never go out in evenings	9	11	25
Out once a week	27	34	37
Out two or more times a week	64	55	38
Base: 100 percent =	(110)	(126)	(102)

The light viewing audience, those watching less than ten hours a week, is composed largely of gad-abouts who go out for the evening at least twice a week; the heavy viewers are much more apt to be stay-at-homes (25 percent as compared to 9 percent of the light viewers). It may seem a rather obvious discovery—that people have to stay at home in order to watch a lot of television—but it is still worth the telling. There is a theory abroad about leisure behavior to the effect that people who are active in some leisure-time activities are apt to be active in others as well. Rolf Meyersohn calls this "the more, the more" hypothesis, and shows that it applies, in some cases.[7] There would appear to be a practical limitation when applied to more television viewing if much of "the more" of other activities takes one out of the house.

But not all alternative activities take people out of the house and it is possible that some of those that do may not affect television viewing in a lessening fashion. The respondents in the Minneapolis–St. Paul sample were asked whether they engaged in some rather specific activities—inside and outside the house—on a more or less regular basis. Those who said they did these things—various proportions of the sample for each one—were again classified into light, average, or heavy viewers of television, as shown in Table 3-20.

Of the four activities on the list which would of necessity take people out of the house, two (going to concerts and plays, and going to meetings, and so on) seem to be associated with light viewing of television, and one (going to movies) is found slightly more among average and heavy viewers. Domestic activities are similarly scattered. Playing musical instruments and listening to recorded music are more apt to be found among people who watch television less, but those who listen to radio or read a newspaper every day and those who entertain at home weekly are apt to watch television just as much as those who do not.

More significant perhaps is the intellectual nature of activities embraced by the lighter viewers of television—the first five on the list. Concerts and plays, music, books, meetings, and lectures suggest an orientation toward the arts and humanities that we associate with the educated and cultured elements of society—close to Meyersohn's idea of a "book culture" that depresses people's attitudes toward television viewing.[8] Here we find some slight evidence that such an orientation may influence the actual amount of time people spend in viewing.

From this brief sketch of television viewers—their time before the set, their characteristics and their methods and motives in viewing—a few general conclusions might be reached. Certainly the audience has increased the amount of time it spends in viewing, according to what the 1960 and 1970 survey respondents say, and, more convincingly, according to the measurements of the rating services. But there is nothing in the data re-

---

[7] Rolf Meyersohn, "Television and the Rest of Leisure," *Public Opinion Quarterly*, Spring 1958, pp. 102–112.
[8] Rolf Meyersohn, *Leisure and Television, op. cit.*

table 3-20
"Now I'd like to ask you some questions about how you spend your leisure time, aside from watching television. Do you *usually* do any of the following things; for instance, on the average do you:

ACTIVITY	Percent Engaging in Various Activities By Amount of Viewing		
	Light Viewers (Less than 10 hrs.)	Average Viewers (10–20 hrs.)	Heavy Viewers (More than 20 hrs.)
1. Go to concerts or plays once a month?	16	8	9
2. Listen to music on records and tapes several times a week?	64	53	50
3. Go to any meetings, lectures, or talks once a month?	54	48	39
4. Read a book at least once a month?	52	48	42
5. Play a musical instrument, once a week?	15	13	12
6. Read something in a magazine every day?	53	45	53
7. Read a newspaper every day?	84	80	85
8. Have people into your house once a week?	73	71	72
9. Listen to the radio practically every day?	86	86	85
10. Go to other peoples' houses once a week?	58	60	56
11. Go to a movie at least twice a month?	7	10	12
BASE: 100 percent =	(110)	(126)	(102)

viewed so far which would suggest that this increase in viewing has resulted from burgeoning enthusiasm for the medium; the observed decline in general attitudes would hardly support such an hypothesis. In point of fact, there is nothing in the data to support much of a relationship *at all* between people's characteristics and the views they hold about television on the one hand, and the amount of time they spend watching it on the other. When we examine our respondents' evening and weekend viewing it turns out that the groups who like television least are watching it about as much as those who like it most.

Among the factors that *do* seem to have some effect on how much television viewing goes on is *opportunity,* in the form of available free time. It is when opportunities are more or less equalized that we find the differences among the subgroups of the population generally nonexistent (as with the AID analysis), and it is more free time that permits the citizens of Minneapolis–St. Paul to increase their viewing, and the lack of free time that causes them to watch less than they did before. The fact that the working time of the American worker declined during the decade, from an average of 38.6 hours per week to an average of 37.1 hours may suggest one contributing factor to the ten-year increase in television watching.[9] Of course, any available free time could be used in any number of leisure-time pursuits, given the desire and the equipment and the will power. So to say that more of it can increase television viewing is to state a necessary condition but hardly a sufficient one. With television viewing taking up as much of America's leisure time as it does today, however, it is a very important necessary condition. Any activity that consumes several hours a day would be particularly vulnerable to variations in the total amount of leisure time available. It may be that time free from inescapable obligations is *the* most important factor in the viewing equation.

The reasons for viewing to which people subscribe form another part of the equation. The respondents' answers suggest relaxation and enjoyment as predominant motives for watching, with some viewers apparently seeking edification, and others apparently moved by a variety of personal needs. All the reasons which people accept, when asked about them (with the possible exception of "viewing for background"), assume some reaction to the *content* of television, which is the subject of the next chapter.

---

[9] *Monthly Labor Review,* U.S. Department of Labor, Bureau of Labor Statistics, October 1972, p. 106.

CHAPTER *4*
REACTIONS
TO PROGRAMS

Some puzzling findings were presented in the last two chapters. During the decade when the amount of time viewers spent watching television sharply increased, their previously high regard for the medium showed something of a decline. And, while the over-all general attitudes toward television were declining, more people than before praised one particular aspect of the medium's performance—its superior ability over the other media in bringing them the news. This leads to a consideration of other aspects of television's programming in search of a reason why some people would seem to be watching it more and appreciating it less. In reviewing the 1960 and 1970 data, we deal with popular views on various broad aspects of the content of television and reactions to some of the changes that have taken place over the ten years.

From the shifts in general attitude previously observed, we might expect that further broad questions about the *content* of television would elicit fewer expressions of appreciation than they had in the previous survey. We asked, as did Steiner, a set of general questions on television programs: what proportion of the programs does the respondent feel are "extremely enjoyable," "somewhat enjoyable," "just so-so-," and "disappointing?" The distributions of the two samples' estimates of "extremely

chart 4-1

Proportion of Programs Felt to Be "Extremely Enjoyable"

"Television programs, like most other things, vary in quality. Some are better than others. Considering just the programs you generally watch, what proportion would you say are extremely enjoyable, how many are somewhat enjoyable, how many are just so-so, and how many are disappointing? First, what percentage of the TV programs you watch would you call 'extremely enjoyable'?"

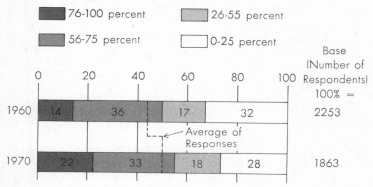

enjoyable" and "disappointing" programs are shown in Charts 4-1 and 4-2 in percentage intervals.

What we see is a general improvement in the public's rating of television programming, despite the opposite shifts in attitudes toward the medium. The percentages have moved *up* since 1960. Using Steiner's

chart 4-2

Proportion of Programs Felt to Be "Disappointing"

"And what percentage of the programs you watch would you call 'disappointing'?"

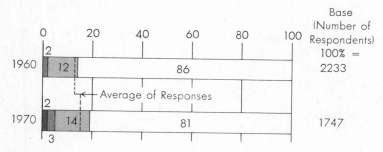

chart 4-3

Average Proportion of Programs Felt to Be "Extremely Enjoyable" (by education)

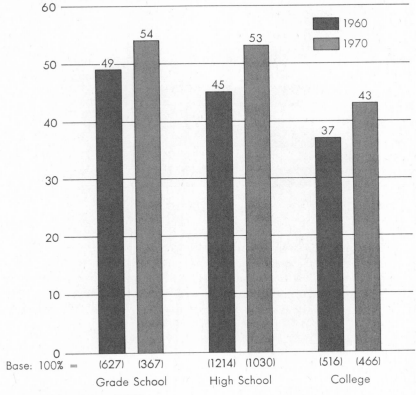

Base: 100% =   (627) (367)   (1214) (1030)   (516) (466)
                Grade School   High School   College

1960 Base: 100% = 2357
1970 Base: 100% = 1887

method of calculating the average of all responses, the figure for the average proportion of all programs found to be "extremely enjoyable" by the 1970 population rose to 50 percent, as compared to 44 percent ten years earlier. There was also a slight shift in the other direction: a larger percentage of the 1970 sample, by a 2 percent average of responses, found programs to be "disappointing."

As it does in attitudes generally, education makes a difference in the rating of programs. In both the 1960 and 1970 surveys, the less-educated respondents said they enjoyed more of their programs than the better educated. The increased 1970 ratings are found in all three educa-

chart 4-4

Proportion of Programs Felt to Be "Extremely Enjoyable"-by Education (1970 respondents)

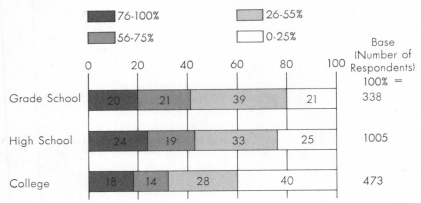

tional groups. These findings are shown in charts 4-3, 4-4, and 4-5: the first (Chart 4-3) shows the general shifts in ratings over the decade, the second (Chart 4-4) shows the components of the 1970 ratings. We see that the college educated do not differ very much from the less educated in their number of enthusiasts (defined here as those who find over three-quarters

chart 4-5

Proportion of Programs Felt to Be "Disappointing"-by Education (1970 respondents)

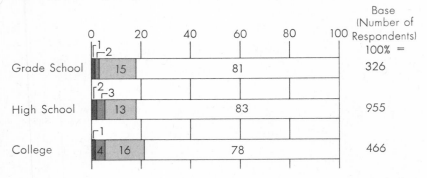

74

of the programs "extremely enjoyable"). Where college *does* matter is in the number of critics it produces—40 percent of the college educated find only a quarter or less of their programs "extremely enjoyable," as compared to 21 percent of those with only a grade school education.

At the other extreme—"disappointing" programs—we see very little differentiation (Chart 4-5). The college educated, as well as those with less education, reject the application of that opprobrium to their programs. So the educated viewers take a middling position. Not very many of them think a high proportion of their programs are "extremely enjoyable" or think a high proportion are "disappointing." For most of them, programs are generally "somewhat enjoyable" or "just so-so."

Both the better and less educated, nevertheless, show the same over-all shift toward greater enjoyment of programs. Similarly, men and women, and the young and old, are part of the general trend. Like the general attitudinal shift, this would appear to be a trend affecting all parts of the society.

REACTIONS TO TYPES OF PROGRAMS

The finding that many programs are more pleasing to the public (educated or not) in 1970 than they were in 1960, can now be followed with a more detailed examination of specific program content to which the public is reacting; looking first at the answers to questions in which people were asked to express their desires about program emphases, and then listening to their own assessments of the changes that have taken place over the decade.

A series of questions in the 1960 survey, repeated in 1970, asked people how much attention they thought television should pay to programs that provided different "things" for them—education, advice, amusement, escape. Answers to these questions and to two others added in the 1970 survey are shown in Table 4-1. The 1960 public said it wanted more educational programs—only on that item did the proportion who wanted more (65 percent saying "not enough") exceed the satisfied customers who thought there were "enough." Otherwise people were pleased with what they were getting, if we may interpret "enough" as a sign of contentment with the available fare. They were especially satisfied with the opportunities for escape—few of them wanted either more or less of that. A third of the sample, however, wanted more laughs and more programs with advice helpful to problem-solving.

The 1970 population is not nearly so complacent. A higher proportion of it—75 percent—now says that there is not enough educational

table 4-1

"Television programs can be designed to provide different things. From your point of view, does television have enough, not enough, or too many of each of these kinds of programs?"

(by education of respondent)

KIND OF PROGRAM	1960 Grade School	High School	Col-lege	1960 Total	1970 Total	1970 Grade School	High School	Col-lege
Educational								
Enough	50	34	16	34	24	32	24	19
Not enough	49	65	83	65	75	66	74	81
Too many	1	—	1	1	1	3	1	—
Base: 100 percent = .	(294)	(616)	(251)	(1161)	(1517)	(238)	(837)	(442)
Escape from Everyday Life								
Enough	84	75	60	74	56	53	59	53
Not enough	9	11	11	11	17	20	19	13
Too many	7	14	29	15	27	28	22	34
Base: 100 percent = .	(291)	(604)	(248)	(1143)	(1343)	(187)	(766)	(390)
Advice or Problem Solving								
Enough	66	61	57	61	35	43	34	31
Not enough	31	33	33	32	58	55	58	60
Too many	4	6	11	6	7	2	8	9
Base: 100 percent = .	(281)	(587)	(228)	(1096)	(1008)	(165)	(557)	(286)
Just Laughs								
Enough	66	63	59	63	61	60	60	62
Not enough	28	33	35	39	32	33	33	29
Too many	6	4	6	5	8	8	7	10
Base: 100 percent = .	(294)	(618)	(249)	(1161)	(1710)	(301)	(955)	(454)
*Information about Social Problems**								
Enough	—	—	—	—	41	47	42	36
Not enough	—	—	—	—	27	16	26	34
Too many	—	—	—	—	32	37	33	29
Base: 100 percent = .	—	—	—	—	(1487)	(226)	(828)	(433)
*Information about Politics and Political Candidates**								
Enough	—	—	—	—	57	60	59	52
Not enough	—	—	—	—	26	17	23	35
Too many	—	—	—	—	18	23	18	13
Base: 100 percent = .	—	—	—	—	(1474)	(241)	(797)	(436)

* Item not included in 1960 Questionnaire.

programming. Have peoples' tastes been whetted by the offerings of educational stations? Escape programs, so much more acceptable before, are now rejected or at least considered too numerous by 27 percent of the public. There are not enough advice programs for 58 percent of the sample. But people still want to laugh; on that one item, the proportions remain the same.

The ten-year differences should not be overinterpreted. There is a fair degree of semantic ambiguity in the questions—people may escape through laughter or tears, or in the excitement of a football game. Some of the responses to a request for examples of programs of which there are "too many" or "not enough" suggest that a wide variety of meanings were attached to the labels given to the program types. In the "advice" area, programs mentioned ranged from Billy Graham's crusade (moral advice) to *The Wide World of Sports* (how to hook a marlin). There is an additional qualification: in 1970, for unknown reasons, a much higher proportion answered "don't know" to these questions. Perhaps if the don't-knowers were pressed to make a choice, they would have swelled the "enough" category.

But clearly, those who did make choices, whatever sorts of programs they had in mind when choosing, did not give the support to the status quo that Steiner found in 1960. There is nothing here to explain the improved general rating of programs as pleasure-givers that we observed earlier.

The answers to the question on educational programs and to the two questions on programs about social problems and politics show a clear relationship to the educational level of the respondents. The better-educated viewers are the ones who want more information about U.S. social problems, more on politics and candidates for office, and more educational fare. This is a relationship we will treat in greater detail in the subsequent chapter on television journalism.

Two questions on program preferences of a rather more specific nature were also included in both surveys. The "specials"—those one-shot video events that can either annoy because they pre-empt the regular programs to which one is addicted, or delight because they are seen as fresh departures from the usual fare—are they to be applauded or condemned? And programs that provide information—should television provide more of those, or should it stick to the area of its early strength and improve its entertainment programming? The advice of the two samples on each of these questions is shown in Tables 4-2 and 4-3.

The public verdict on the first question has changed since 1960. The vote then clearly favored the regularly scheduled shows over the specials (49 percent to 32 percent); in 1970, a plurality favored the specials. This increase in popularity of the specials is found in each educa-

table 4-2

"In general do you think that specials or spectaculars are better than the regular shows they replace or would you rather see the regularly scheduled programs?"

(by education of respondents)

PERCENT WHO SAY:	1960				1970			
	Grade School	High School	Col- lege	1960 Total	1970 Total	Grade School	High School	Col- lege
Regular shows better ...	59	53	32	49	36	48	43	23
Specials better	19	31	50	32	44	26	39	60
No difference	23	16	18	19	19	26	18	18
Base: 100 percent = .	(627)	(1214)	(516)	(2357)	(1887)	(367)	(1030)	(440)

tional group but is most pronounced among the better educated, which, in 1970 make up a higher proportion of the total population.

A similar relationship with education pervades the 1960 and 1970 choices between informational material and entertainment; the higher the educational level, the larger the vote for information. But the outcome— a plurality victory in entertainment in both years—is confounded by a discrepancy in the two surveys' procedures. In 1960 when a respondent

table 4-3

"Generally speaking would you say that television should provide more informational material or should it concentrate on providing the best entertainment possible?"

(by education of respondent)

PERCENT WHO SAY:	1960				1970			
	Grade School	High School	Col- lege	1960 Total	1970 Total	Grade School	High School	Col- lege
Provide more informa- tional material	27	28	40	31	24	19	23	32
Provide best entertainment	48	43	25	40	38	41	42	27
Both, can't choose don't know	25	29	36	29	38	41	35	41
Base: 100 percent = .	(621)	(1204)	(510)	(2335)	(1843)	(347)	(1018)	(478)

said "both," he was asked by the interviewer: "well, suppose there was a free hour on the air that could be used for any kind of program at all, what would you like to see it used for?" The extra opportunity thus provided to make a choice was apparently grasped more by the less educated, who would tend to opt for entertainment, and resisted by the college group who are more apt to favor information. If we had added this probe too in 1970, we might have found an increased vote for entertainment in the total sample, but the educational differences would have remained.

One might have thought that the request for more educational material, high in 1960 and even higher in 1970 (Table 4-1), could have been met by the increased number of educational television programs on public broadcasting stations. However, for the purely technical reasons discussed in the last chapter, sizable proportions of viewers are deprived of ETV. And the better educated, those whom we now see to be the ones who want more educational material—were better able to receive the educational channels. Among all the viewers who can receive an educational television channel *and* say that they watch it, 77 percent still say that there are not enough programs with educational material; of those who can receive but don't watch, 74 percent say there are not enough.

It would appear that ETV has either failed to satisfy a need that many of its own viewers express or that it has so stimulated the appetite for education that more of it is demanded. But there is the third possibility—that a perceptual gulf exists between what the viewers think ETV provides and what they feel they need when they ask for more educational material on television generally. Some evidence for this proposition is found among the answers to the interviewers' requests for "the kind of program you have in mind when you say there are not enough programs providing educational material."

A sampling of the responses revealed a wide range of interests and levels of sophistication regarding educational programming. For example, some respondents referred to specific programs of the sort educational channels carry, such as *Sesame Street*, foreign news analysis, and science and math instruction. Many respondents referred to more general programming *themes*, such as travel programs and programs on foreign cultures and geography, while others indicated documentaries, "specials," or such series as *Jacques Cousteau, First Tuesday* and *60 Minutes*. A few respondents were even more specific in their requests for programs which would fulfill their particular personal needs, mentioning such subjects as home repairs, preparation of income-tax forms, and cooking and sewing programs. It would appear that a large proportion of the public feels the need to endorse "education," but that the exact meaning of the term

79

varies considerably. On the whole, the term "educational" appears to refer to any subject that requires a certain amount of concentration and involvement on the part of the viewer rather than to mere superficial entertainment; beyond that, a wide variety of programs would apparently be considered educational by much of the viewing public.

WHAT THEY WANTED AND WHAT THEY GOT

A look at programming changes that have occurred in all broadcasting over ten years shows that some people got what they wanted, others did not. The requests for more news and information were fulfilled, those for more comedy were not. As a quantitative measure of these changes, we have only a rather crude index—the distribution of broadcasting time spent on eleven types of programs in two cities, New York and Minneapolis–St Paul. Probably neither one of these cities individually, nor both combined, represent accurately the total national television broadcasting in 1960 or 1970; but large over-all changes in programming would be reflected to some extent in the programs they offered.

The eleven categories of programs that Steiner used in 1960 and which we repeat in 1970, include six types of light entertainment: *Comedy/Variety*, for example Red Skelton and Ed Sullivan in 1960 and Red Skelton and Laugh-in in 1970; *Action* (Gunsmoke, Ironside, The Young Lawyers); *Movies*, except for "serious" movies such as a Shakespearean tragedy; *Light Drama* (Marcus Welby or the soap operas); *Light Music* (popular); and *Sports. Heavy entertainment* (for example, *classical music* and *heavy drama*), *Regular News, Information and Public Affairs* and *Réligion* complete the list of categories.

Table 4-4 shows the total distribution of time devoted to various types of programs in unduplicated minutes (two half-hour news programs in the same time period are counted as one half-hour of news programming).[1] One of the differences between 1960 and 1970—the increase in information and public affairs broadcasting—is partly explained by the inclusion of educational TV broadcasting in 1970. In 1960, neither city had an ETV channel; in 1970 we included the VHF–Minneapolis educational channel in the tabulations but restricted our New York City count to stations that had been included in Steiner's tallies. Among other differences of significance to the viewer, movies consume a large part of entertainment program time in both years, but more of them in 1970 appeared in prime-time early evening hours when the television audience is at its

---

[1] See Appendix C.

largest. There were also marked shifts in content within some of the categories. Westerns, for instance, are a much smaller component of the "Action" category in 1970 than they were in 1960.

table 4-4

"What kinds of programs have you seen that you'd like to see more often on TV? Can you give an example?"

Distribution of Programming in Two Cities and 1960 Program Desires

	Programming in Unduplicated Minutes		1960 Program Desires
	1960	1970	
Light Entertainment			
Comedy/variety	22	21	25
Movies	20	18	1
Action	18	16	16
Sports	9	9	7
Light music	4	5	11
Light drama	9	3	8
News and Information			
Regular news	5	10	1
Information and public affairs	8	14	19
Heavy Drama	4	2	7
Religion	2	3	5
Heavy Music	0	0	1
Base: 100 percent = ...	(19950)	(29055)	(2160)

Over all, the shift appears to have been slightly *away* from light entertainment programs (from 82 percent down to 72 percent) and *toward* news, information and public affairs (from 13 percent, up to 24 percent).

Television, judging by our measurements, did not quite redistribute the total time it devoted to various program types in 1970 so as to fulfill the requests of the 1960 public. A large proportion of the latter (25 percent) might have been willing to sacrifice other things to have more comedy and variety shows, but that category remains rather stable in 1970. On the other hand, the 1960 request for more information and public affairs programs is matched by increased programming available in that area. Whether on ETV or on the commercial channels, there are more information shows on the air now for those who said they would like more of them in 1960.

     With limitless expansion of the industry—more channels to watch and a greater variety of programs to choose from at any one time— everybody's wishes could theoretically be met. At the moment, however, we are concerned with the actual changes during the decade as they relate to the changes in attitudes we are observing. One may assume, on that score, that not everybody should be equally pleased—that the redistribution of available programs was more in accord with the desires of some than of others. Table 4-5 is based on answers to a second Steiner question in which he asked about favorite programs. The proportions of each educational group who chose light entertainment and who chose news, information, or public affairs programs are shown so that they may

table 4-5

"What are some of your favorite programs—those you watch regularly or whenever you get a chance?"

Comparison of Favorite Program Types in 1960 (by Education of Respondent) with Program Type Availability in 1960 and 1970

	Grade School	High School	College	1960	1970
				Proportion of Total Unduplicated Broadcasting Minutes Available by Program Types	
Favorite Program Types—1960					
Light entertainment	87	87	66	82	72
News, information and public affairs	8	9	22	13	24
Base: 100 percent = ..	(627)	(1214)	(516)	1960 base: 100 percent = 19950 unduplicated minutes 1970 base: 100 percent = 29055 unduplicated minutes	

be compared to the changes in actual programming in these two broad categories.

The new program distributions appear to favor the better-educated viewer, whose favorite programs were more apt to be in the news and information areas and less in light entertainment. Whether in 1970 he took advantage of the opportunities that were available to him is the subject of a subsequent chapter.

THE COMMERCIALS

Gary Steiner commented, while reviewing his 1960 data on popular reactions to advertising on television, that the average viewer has probably not given much thought to commercial sponsorship as a system for financing broadcasting nor has he considered its alternatives. His data showed a high degree of acceptance of advertising when people were asked whether they agreed or disagreed with a series of statements about it. Most people agreed that commercials were "a fair price to pay for the entertainment you get." Over half found them helpful in keeping informed, many thought they were as entertaining as the programs themselves and over a third even found themselves frequently welcoming a commercial break. Somewhat less than half the sample said they would prefer television without commercials and even fewer (24 percent) said they would be willing to pay in order to eliminate the ads. It is not that everybody had only praise for commercials—which were too long for most and deemed to be in bad taste by many—but the over-all positive reactions tended to outweigh negative ones.

If ten years later the average viewer can imagine an alternative and more satisfactory way of financing his viewing, there is little indication of that in his answers to the same series of questions. He is, at most, only *slightly* more negative now. Five percent more of the sample now prefer TV without commercials and 6 percent more say they would be willing to pay for it. Again the commercials are felt to be too long, and in response to a new item, are found to be too frequent. But this small indication of a trend is countered by a higher proportion in 1970 than in 1960 finding "some commercials . . . more entertaining than the program." The average viewer still overwhelmingly accepts the frequent and long interruptions by commercials as a "fair price to pay"; three-fourths of the sample accepted them in 1960, 70 percent in 1970.

There is another interesting similarity between the findings of the two surveys. Steiner noted that the reactions to commercials did not vary much among segments of the audience. The two sexes and people of

83

table 4-6

"Here are some statements about commercials. I'd like you to read each statement and mark whether you generally agree or disagree with each statement."

PERCENT WHO AGREE THAT:	1960 Total	1970 Total	1970 Occupation of Head of Household	
			White Collar	Blue Collar
Commercials are a fair price to pay for the entertainment you get	75	70	69	71
Most commercials are too long	63	65	67	65
I find some commercials very helpful in keeping me informed	58	54	50	57
Some commercials are so good that they are more entertaining than the program	43	54	56	52
I would prefer TV without commercials	43	48	49	47
Commercials are generally in poor taste and very annoying	40	43	42	43
I frequently find myself welcoming a commercial break	36	35	31	38
I'd rather pay a small amount yearly to have TV without commercials	24	30	30	29
There are just too many commercials	(Not included in 1960)	70	71	70
Having special commercial breaks during a program is better than having the same number of commercials at the beginning and end	(Not included in 1960)	39	35	42
Base: 100 percent = ...	(2427)	(1900)	(674)	(873)

84

table 4-7

"Are there any products or types of things now advertised on TV that you think should not be advertised on television?" "What are they?"

PERCENT WHO MENTIONED:	Grade School	High School	College	Total
Cigarettes, tobacco	30	33	39	34
Liquor, beer, "booze"	15	16	15	16
Personal undergarments	2	6	8	6
Personal hygiene products	2	5	9	5
Drugs and medicine	5	4	7	5
Soaps and detergents	5	3	4	4
Other	4	3	3	4
Base: 100 percent = ...	(368)	(1030)	(490)	(1888)

different ages felt similarly; even the critical socioeconomic variables, such as education, produced only modest differences (the better educated were more critical of commercials). Table 4-6 shows the 1970 population split into two occupational groups. The blue-collar workers, for which one may read poorer and less educated, and the white-collar workers give almost identical answers to most of the items.

We probed deeper and rather pointedly in 1970 for criticism of the commercials, asking our sample first whether there are any products which they think should not be advertised on television at all, and then whether they had objections to the *way* in which things are advertised. Both questions evoked responses from less than half the sample—the first question, 47 percent and the second, 39 percent. Answers to the first question are shown in Table 4-7, by educational group.

It is not surprising that in 1970 tobacco led the list of products to be banned. The relationship between cigarette smoking and cancer had been established and the government interdiction against tobacco advertising had already been announced at the time of the interview. Liquor was second, among both the better- and less-educated respondents. The affronts to one's sense of privacy that may have been behind the objections to a display of undergarments and articles of personal hygiene (especially deodorants) seem to affect the better educated to a greater degree.[2]

---

[2] According to Broadcast Advertisers Reports, Inc., *food, alcoholic beverages, toiletries* and *drugs* account for about half of all network TV billings. *Fortune*, January 1971, p. 87.

85

With our second question, about other objectionable features of commercials, we can make a rough comparison with answers to a 1960 survey item in which the respondents were asked what they "dislike most about commercials" (see Table 4-8). The two questions, so differently worded, can provide only a crude indication of changes in emphasis on objectionable features. The 1960 wording evoked many more responses about the commercials' length and frequency than did the phraseology used in 1970.

Within these limitations, we may still point to a relative increase since 1960 in the accusations of "bad taste," a category of response that includes "vulgarity" and "suggestiveness." Let us hear from a few of the 1970 respondents on this score:

"Yes. The ideas that suggest that people are living together without being married; also instilling in young people, the idea that if they use certain products they're going to become instant movie stars."

"Yes. I object to the using of a beautiful woman to sell almost everything, especially the way they dress them—bikinis, see-through outfits. They should be able to sell products without using beautiful women for selling things."

"Those bathing suit models. I don't like nudity on TV. Bathing

table 4-8

1960: "What, if anything, do you dislike most about commercials?"
1970: "Aside from the things advertised, is there anything that goes on in commercials that you object to?" "What do you object to?"
(By Education of Respondent)

PERCENT WHO MENTION:	1960				1970			
	Grade School	High School	Col-lege	1960 Total	1970 Total	Grade School	High School	Col-lege
Misleading, dishonest	11	15	20	16	8	6	7	12
Bad taste, suggestive	6	8	13	8	15	12	14	19
Stupid, unrealistic, silly . . .	5	10	18	11	15	8	16	17
Boring, dull	13	18	20	17	1	—	2	1
Hard sell, aggressive	3	4	7	5	2	1	2	2
Base: 100 percent = . . .	(627)	(1214)	(516)	(2427)	(1888)	(368)	(1030)	(490)

86

beauties are for the beach not on a TV commercial to sell men's hair dressing."

"Don't like piggy-back commercials. Neither do I like so much sex in commercials. They can't let a person brush their teeth in a commercial without some sex in it."

"Every commercial has to have sex in it some way. It has to be brought in somewhere. Something has got to be suggestive. I resent having to do without TV in order to protect my children from these things."

Fewer of the 1970 sample found commercials dull or boring, but just about as many as in the past find them unrealistic and silly, or at least unconvincing:

"Yes. Some ads promise utopia and this is impossible. An example is like advertising toothpaste and promising boy will get girl. This is too misleading for young people."

"Yes. Most of the time it is ridiculous, silly and mentally annoying. There are many, I can't think of one. Yes, a bank, with all its dignity, has a sketch of two houses with mouths, each opening and getting messages across. Silly."

"Some of them are silly. They are an insult to your intelligence. Those where they have a blouse with unbearable stains and they wash it and it comes out clean."

So a minority distinctly finds objectionable features in commercials. More people than in the past are offended by what they see as vulgarity, a theme that appears in the answers of more parents (18 percent) than of nonparents (12 percent). However, the majority finds no objection, some even find praise. Most appear still willing to accept commercials as an immutable fact of life.

PERCEPTION OF CHANGES

So far, this chapter has reviewed several aspects of television content about which the public has altered its reactions—or failed to do so—over a ten-year period. Not much has been discovered to explain the finding of higher public assessment of programs as enjoyable. We may have missed some pieces to the puzzle in using ten-year old items from Steiner's questionnaire; they were phrased to capture the popular feelings of an earlier decade, and could not have anticipated new elements in television's total content to which the public now may have significant reactions. Even if Steiner *had* anticipated some content changes, such as programs beamed from abroad by satellite or the expansion of ETV, it would not have done much good to ask about them if the public was unaware of their possible existence. He did, as a matter of fact, ask about educational television, but very few in the sample had anything to say about it.

To correct this deficiency somewhat, we asked the 1970 respondents a few questions about their own views on changes in television over ten years, starting with a broad open-ended question—what new things had they noticed?—and continuing with inquiries about how they viewed specific changes in television, which we took the liberty of noticing for them.

The first open-ended question received a wide variety of replies on several different dimensions, as is the wont of questions of this sort. Some people talked about specific programs, others about technical features and still others about new themes they perceived as pervading television's content. The answers were classified variously, as can be seen in the following tabulations in Table 4-9.

table 4-9

"Now how about changes that have taken place in TV over the past ten years? What do you see as some of the important changes that have taken place?"

OVER-ALL DIRECTION OF REPLY

	Percent
Favorable	55
Unfavorable	16
Neutral, balanced, NA	29

TYPES OF REPLIES

	Percent
Mentioned Favorably:	
News and information	33
Technical changes	23
General entertainment	19
Mentioned Unfavorably:	
Morality themes	10
Violence	4
Favorable, Unfavorable and Neutral Mentions:	
Movies	7
Sports	5
Other Replies and NA	24

Base: 100 percent = 1900

The changes people said they had noticed were described in predominantly laudatory tones. Fifty-five percent of the sample had only good things to say compared with 16 percent who spoke only negatively. The remainder saw both good and bad or limited their replies to neutral comments.

Changes noticed in three categories were seen as changes for the better; the regular news, educational programs, information features were generally all improvements, except in the opinion of a few who didn't like what the news told them about the state of the world. Technical changes —such as more programs in color, better reception or more channels to watch—were hardly ever viewed with disfavor; and the new entertainment features were generally praised, except when they contained too much of a worrisome theme such as sex.

People generally felt neutral about ten-year changes in sports programs and movies; the men seemed to like what they saw in sports, and both sexes appreciated the movies except when they were too risqué.

Two distinctly negative themes emerged with some frequency in the answers. The accusation of "more violence" or "too much violence shown now" was often accompanied by comments about events covered by television news—the Vietnam War or riots in the streets. The morality themes, on the other hand—sex, nudity, vulgarity—are found in old movies and advertisements and in the regular entertainment programs. When discussed, they are often accompanied by comments concerning their effects on children.

Here are a few of the answers that our respondents gave to this question. First, some favorable ones.

"They don't have as many criminal shows on. Less horror shows and cartoons. They have more educational programs. Much more news. They show so much more of happenings—conventions, riots, the war. You feel as though you're right there as a part of it."

"They're up to the minute with news coverage. The fuller coverage of sports. More live shows."

"I think they no longer assume the public is stupid and are upgrading and informing people better than they were ten years ago."

"It is more worldwide in scope than it was ten years ago. It is truly amazing what they can do with TV. For instance, the moon-walk telecast. It was really an event that will go down in history."

Here are two neutral or ambivalent answers:

"One significant change is that it's a little more liberal and not so restricted as ten years ago. There are more news documentaries but less live television. There are more sports on TV too."

"More complete coverage of current events and a lessening of the moral programming code. Marvelous coverage about scientific things—especially the moon shots."

And some unfavorable ones:

"The important thing is that it is going down. Our 16-year-old will never have to go to a burlesque show because he has already seen it on TV. Variety shows have it all. Everything is trash. I can't sit down and relax and watch a TV show without being on the alert to see if it is going to be all right for the children. They downgrade our intelligence. We have more college graduates and lower morals than ever before."

"Some of the programs aren't as good as they were ten years ago, I tell you. They're not as interesting as they were to me. Too much roughness, sex and crude stuff. Don't care at all what they say. That's not good for little kids to see and hear."

"There is more news. Vietnam and other worldly news. There is more about murders and killings. There is more about sex in everything but the news. In the movies they show more open sex than ever before. It surely isn't so good for young people to see so much of sex everywhere—TV, magazines, movies, etc."

"More vulgar programs are on, more brazen things go on in the shows, more brazen things in newspapers and magazines now too, it's not all in TV."

There were some people who did not see any changes at all and were not too happy about it:

"I can't see any change. I don't think the programs are any better. They are still showing old-time movies from years ago that I saw when I was a girl. They always show what they think people want to see. The commentators are too biased in their opinions, but they have always been like that."

"I don't think there are any changes. It has the same kind of monkey business they had all the time. I don't see any difference, it is all about the same."

A striking general feature of the answers to these questions was the extent to which the journalistic functions of television were emphasized.

News, information, and public affairs programs together consume less than a quarter of total broadcasting time. Yet more people noticed changes in these areas than in entertainment programming, which commands a far greater share of stations' television day and of the audience's time spent before the sets.

This point is made again by the answers to two different but related questions (Table 4-10).

table 4-10

"How about the entertainment programs during the evenings after 7:30 as compared to ten years ago. Do you think they have gotten better, worse, or stayed about the same?"

	Percent Who Say
Better	48
Worse	12
Stayed the same	32
Don't know	8
Base: 100 percent =	1849

"Compared to ten years ago, do you think that the way the news is presented on TV is generally better or generally worse, or has it stayed about the same?"

	Percent Who Say
Better	69
Worse	7
Stayed the same	19
Don't know	5
Base: 100 percent =	1855

The answers to both these questions are generally favorable to the medium. The number of people who see entertainment programs as having "stayed the same," however, is fairly high—32 percent of the sample. Combined with the "don't knows" (who also presumably detected little change), this amounts to 40 percent of the sample, compared with 24 percent of the sample who thought that news presentation had stayed the same or did not remember if it had. People also evaluate the changes they see in news presentation more highly (ten-to-one for "better" over "worse") than they do the entertainment changes (four-to-one for "better"). Relatively, entertainment appears as the less creative portion of television's menu, and its new dishes are less tasty.

Having received the respondent's opening testimony on changes without much prodding, we then asked him to evaluate some very specific changes—all matters of empirical record—which we claimed quite truthfully that others had noticed. They undoubtedly do not represent all the changes that have taken place over a ten-year period, but they do cover just about everything that the respondents had spontaneously noted (except for themes of morality, and violence, which would have been difficult to phrase as uncontrovertible truths).

Items in the Table 4-11 are ordered by degree of approval, so it is easy to see where people saw the greatest and the least improvement. Live coverage of national events, educational television, more channels, television by satellite, and longer news programs are all viewed as changes for the better by 70 percent or more of the sample. At the other end, talk shows, fewer westerns and live coverage of civil disruptions are approved by only about a third. Looking at the two "live coverage" items found on the top and bottom of the list, one can assume that people are responding to the message at least as much as to the medium. Probably it is the space effort that people like and the riots that they dislike. The two items do not serve very well as measures of people's appreciation of news programming generally, but they provide interesting data for Chapter 5 which covers television journalism.

Aside from the degree of approval of each of the changes, it is important to notice the varying number of people who seem not to care; the proportion saying the changes "made no difference" ranges from 8 to 36 percent. This may be used as a crude measure of how salient the changes are to people's evaluation of television's improvement or deterioration over the years; a small percentage saying "no difference" indicates a relatively salient item. By this measure, four items associated with the general area of news and information are highly salient—the two involving live coverage of national events (space and protests), on-the-spot war coverage, and the increase in educational channels. All of the changes in the entertainment area—movies, talk shows, westerns, sports—score low on saliency. This tends to confirm the earlier open testimony of our respondents who on their own noted more of the former types of changes and fewer of the latter.

Answers to our questions about changes tend to show that generally people approve of most of what has taken place in television broadcasting. It is hardly a surprising finding, since all of the technical changes (color TV, more channels, broadcasting by satellite) and many of the changes in content (educational broadcasting, more news) would be hard to find objectionable. We would have suspected, furthermore, that a population

table 4-11

"Here are some ways others have noted that TV has changed over the past ten years. Please tell me, so far as your own TV viewing is concerned, whether this has been a change for the *better*, a change for the *worse* or hasn't it made any difference to you?"

PERCENT WHO SAY:

	Change for Better	Change for Worse	No Dif- ference	Don't Know
More live coverage of important national events, like space shots, etc.	82	6	9	3
More educational channels and more programs on them	78	2	12	7
More channels to watch	75	2	19	4
Programs that are beamed by satellite	70	3	16	11
Longer news programs in the evening..	70	8	19	4
More programs in color	66	0	23	11
More on-the-spot war coverage; for instance, the war in Vietnam	61	21	12	6
Editorials on TV	60	9	22	10
More full-length movies in the evening now than there were before	58	8	27	6
More sports coverage on the weekends	57	16	23	5
More programs with blacks in important roles	48	17	28	7
Fewer westerns than there were before.	36	28	31	5
More talk shows, like Johnny Carson or Merv Griffin	35	20	36	9
More live coverage of disruptions in the U.S., like riots and protests in the streets	34	53	8	5

Base: 100 percent = total sample (excluding NA's which vary from item to item. Total base varies from 1845–1856).

that basically has a high regard for the medium would be somewhat predisposed to accept its innovations.

We would expect also the reverse of that proposition to be true. If people approve of the changes they see taking place, they might tend to have a higher regard for television in general. There should at least be some relationship between approval-of-change and attitude-toward-television, as measured in our study by scores on the attitudinal items discussed previously.

It turns out that evaluations of most of the changes correlate positively with attitudes toward television—the TV fans approve of the changes slightly more than the critics. Only four of the items show a very slight *negative* correlation—fewer westerns, more educational programs, live coverage of space events, and television by satellite. On the other hand, the items also tend to correlate positively with education; the higher educated, who are apt to be critics of television, approve of the changes more than the less educated. If we take all fourteen items together to form a composite *approval-of-change* score, and cross-tabulate that score against *general attitudes toward television*, and against *education*, we find the above relationships again. The TV fans and the better-educated viewers show higher scores on approval-of-change.

There is no way of determining the direction of causality between the two attitudinal variables of approval-of-change and attitudes-toward television. Attitudes toward television could condition the perceptions of changes and views about the changes could alter attitudes, or both could happen. Without attempting to solve this causal relationship, we can still examine further the association of these two attitudinal areas by interjecting the third variable, education, which is associated with both. In Chart 4-6, the three variables are shown in their interrelationships. Scores for approval of changes were developed as follows: Each of the 14 items in the question eliciting attitudes toward various changes in television since 1960 was scored "0" if response was "change for the worse," "1" if response was "no difference" or "don't know," and "2" if response was "change for the better." Scores can range from 0-28.

Let us look first at the lowest and highest educational groups. At the grade school level, all segments tend to have a relatively *low* score on approval of television's changes, regardless of whether they are fans or critics of television. At all three attitudinal levels, the higher percentages are found among the better-educated groups. It would appear that the viewers with only a grade school education are more critical of the changes regardless of how much they love the medium in general. At the other extreme, among the college population, all segments tend to approve the changes, regardless of how they feel about television in general. The TV fans among the college educated show a greater degree of approval than the critics, but even the latter lean in the direction of approval rather than disapproval of the changes. In the middle, among the high school group, the reactions are mixed. The TV fans tend to ap-

chart 4-6

Approval of Changes by Attitude toward Television and Education of Respondent

APPROVAL OF CHANGES:

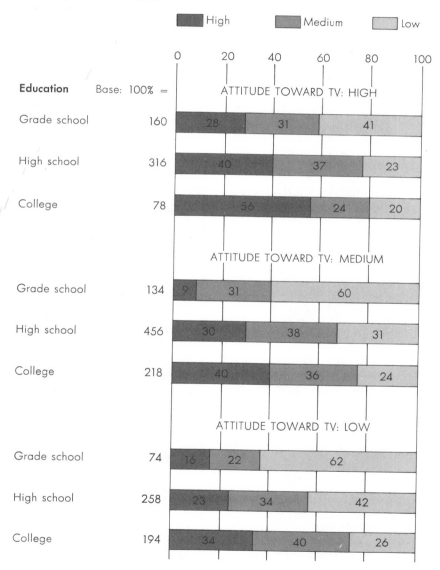

| | | High | Medium | Low |

Education   Base: 100% =

ATTITUDE TOWARD TV: HIGH

	Base: 100% =	High	Medium	Low
Grade school	160	28	31	41
High school	316	40	37	23
College	78	56	24	20

ATTITUDE TOWARD TV: MEDIUM

Grade school	134	9	31	60
High school	456	30	38	31
College	218	40	36	24

ATTITUDE TOWARD TV: LOW

Grade school	74	16	22	62
High school	258	23	34	42
College	194	34	40	26

95

prove of the changes somewhat more than those with lower attitudes toward television.

This all tends to confirm the proposition that a strong relationship exists between education and approval of the changes, and it is one that persists regardless of the people's general attitudes toward the medium. It lends credence to another proposition: the changes that have taken place over the last ten years in television broadcasting have tended to favor the better-educated viewer. If one can conceive of the changes as having been calculated to reach the lowest common denominator, in line with an old accusation leveled at the industry, then they missed the mark. For it is not the traditional TV fan, drawn from the group of less-educated Americans, who is pleased with what has been happening; it is the college man or woman, the critic of the medium, who seems happiest with television's altered condition.

THE BIGGEST MOMENT

As mentioned before, the changes that have caught the attention of television viewers, and of the educated viewers especially, lie less in the field of standard entertainment and more in the areas of programs that inform,

table 4-12

1960: "Considering everything you've ever seen on television, is there some highlight or special moment that stands out in your mind? It can be either a whole program or event or something that happened during a program—just anything that impressed you. What was it?"

1970: "Can you think of the one biggest moment on television for you—the time you would have missed TV the most if you could not have watched what was on? What was it?"

PERCENT WHO SAY:	1960	PERCENT WHO SAY:	1970
No, there isn't, DK, NA	48	No, I can't, DK, NA	37
Episodes or programs in regular entertainment series	24	Episodes or programs in regular entertainment series	5
News coverage of special events	11	JFK assassination and subsequent coverage	12
Documentaries	7	Satellite shots, space phenomenon	35
Informational shows	6	Other news and information	5
Other news and information	4	Other	1
Base: 100 percent = 2427		Base: 100 percent = 1900	

enlighten, and educate. In the next chapter we shall deal specifically with the journalistic section of TV programming, to which our respondents directed our attention by their answers to our questions. But before proceeding to that, we might look at one more piece of evidence of the shift of public attention away from television as the entertainer.

In the 1960 survey, a question was asked of everybody about his or her biggest moment on television. We asked a similar question in 1970 but worded it differently in hope of eliciting a larger response.

Our altered wording of the 1970 question may be responsible for some of the response differences in the two surveys. The word "event" and the implication of dependence in "would have missed" may both have evoked thoughts about news events; the 1960 emphasis on "program" may have led to memories of regular entertainment features. But it is hard to believe that the change in terminology by itself could have had enough force to explain the obvious difference in the two sets of answers: where in 1960 people referred to happenings in television's regular entertainment world more than to anything else, in 1970 only 5 percent of the sample mentioned anything in the arena of standard entertainment. Outstanding moments for the public of 1970 are clearly the national events covered by the television news cameras—especially the victorious conquest of space.

Which leads us to the next chapter.

CHAPTER 5

THE NEWS
ON TELEVISION

By 1960, television had surpassed three other media—newspapers, maga-zines, and radio—as the entertainer of America. Ten years later, without relinquishing that role, it appears to have taken over as America's prime source of current information as well, at least as far as we can tell from our survey. A cautionary note is sounded by findings of a recent study by John Robinson on people's use of TV as a primary news source. He analyzed diary data collected by W. R. Simmons in 1969 showing that 53 percent of the population did not watch a single evening news show during a two-week diary period and that 78 percent of the population reported reading the newspaper on an average day compared with less than 25 percent watching the evening national news on TV.[1] In answers to our survey ques-tions about the four media we find television surging ahead of newspapers during the decade as the news medium that "gives the most complete news coverage," overtaking radio in bringing "the latest news most quickly," edging out newspapers in "presenting the fairest, most unbiased news," and increasing its lead as the medium that "gives the clearest understand-

---

[1] John P. Robinson, "The Audience for National TV News Programs," *Public Opinion Quarterly*, Fall 1971, pp. 403–405.

table 5-1

"Now, I would like to get your opinions about how radio, newspapers, television and magazines compare. Generally speaking, which of these would you say . . ."

		Percent 1960	1970
"Gives the most complete news coverage?"	Television	19	41
	Magazines	3	4
	Newspapers	59	39
	Radio	18	14
	None or Don't Know	1	2
"Brings you the latest news most quickly?"	Television	36	54
	Magazines	0	0
	Newspapers	5	6
	Radio	57	39
	None or Don't Know	2	1
"Gives the fairest, most unbiased news?"	Television	29	33
	Magazines	9	9
	Newspapers	31	23
	Radio	22	19
	None or Don't know	9	16
"Gives the clearest under- standing of candidates and issues in national elections?"	Television	42	59
	Magazines	16	8
	Newspapers	36	21
	Radio	5	3
	None or Don't Know	1	9

1960 Base: 100 percent = 2427 (minus NAs which vary from item to item)
1970 Base: 100 percent = 1900 (minus NAs which vary from item to item)

ing of candidates and issues in national elections." Answers to the four questions are summarized in Table 5-1.

As a trend over a decade, these findings parallel the results of a series of national studies commissioned by the Television Information Office and conducted by the Roper Organization over the years since 1959.[2] In 1959 television trailed newspapers by 51 to 57 percent as the

---

[2] Roper Research Associates, "Emerging Profiles of Television and Other Mass Media: Public Attitudes 1959–1967," Television Information Office, New York, 1959–1967; and Roper Organization Survey, Television Information Office, New York, 1971.

source of "most of your news" (the question allowed people to choose more than one answer). In 1971, in response to the same question, 60 percent favored television, 48 percent newspapers. On another question, in which people were asked to judge the "most believable" medium among the four in situations where reports conflicted, television as the most believable went from 29 percent in 1959, three percentage points behind newspapers, to 49 percent in 1971, 29 percentage points ahead. In both years, and on both questions, radio and magazines trailed behind the other media. Another study by Harvey Jacobson of Wisconsin, in 1966, showed television to be rated ahead of newspapers and radio on a series of qualities including "accuracy," "completeness," "trustworthiness," and "open-mindedness."[3]

The new prominence of television as a news medium has hardly gone unnoticed by students of mass communications. Some of the major foci of the continuing discussions and debates about the role of television in society have shifted in a way that parallels the shift in public views of television from mainly an entertainment medium to both an entertainment and an information medium. In 1960 we were still in the midst of what was then known as "The Big Debate" about television—can the new technology be put to benign humanistic uses, to inform the viewer, enlighten the public, raise the cultural standards of the nation? Or, must it inevitably seek the lowest common denominator in order to engage the attention of the largest possible audience, serving up vacuous entertainment programs so as to achieve that end? At the rhetorical apex of The Big Debate, FCC Commissioner Newton Minow said in his much quoted "vast wasteland" speech: "When television is bad, nothing is worse." Inviting the public to look at television for a day—all day, without interruption—he said assuredly that "you will observe a vast wasteland." In this nothingness, according to Minow, there is a procession of game shows, violence, sadism, murder, gangsters, more violence, and cartoons. There are also commercials, he added, endless commercials. "But most of all, boredom."[4]

During the decade of the sixties television changed, and the debate shifted its ground. Now with their eye focused on TV news programs, the proponents and critics of commercial television argued questions about the function of news and public information in democratic national life—objectivity of reporting, thoroughness of coverage, concentration of control over dissemination and the potential, for good or evil, of television

---

[3] Harvey Jacobson, "Mass Media Believability: A Study of Receiver Judgments," *Journalism Quarterly*, Spring 1969, pp. 20–28.

[4] Speech by Newton Minow on May 9, 1961 before the 39th Annual Convention of the National Association of Broadcasters, Washington, D.C.

news coverage to affect the behavior of its audiences. Vice President Spiro Agnew, the Newton Minow of 1969, dealt with such issues in his Des Moines, Iowa, speech on November 13. Television news, he said, with "its concentration in the hands of a tiny, enclosed fraternity of privileged men, decides what 40 to 50 million Americans will learn of the day's events in the nation and the world. The newsmen can make or break by their coverage and commentary, a Moratorium on the war, [they] can elevate men from obscurity to national prominence within a week. They can reward some politicians with national exposure and ignore others." While deploring this pervasive and concentrated power, the Vice President questioned the objectivity of television, particularly in respect to the news programs' reactions to President Nixon's Laos invasion speech, and criticized television news for its fascination with the disruptive and abnormal —rioters, black radicals—at the expense of the normal and consensual. Toward the end of his speech Agnew called upon the people to "let the networks know that they want their news straight and objective."[5]

    In this chapter we will examine some data from our study that bear on these and related issues, listening to what the public had to say about television journalism when they were interviewed three months after Agnew's speech.

OBJECTIVITY IN THE NEWS

The issue of bias in news reporting, especially political news, is undoubtedly as old as journalism itself, and persists as a continuing concern of conscientious journalists, students, and critics of journalism. Rarely has the question of bias been raised so prominently as just prior to our 1970 interviews, when the Vice President vigorously and at length vented his displeasure with television network news. His speech and the rejoinders to it received wide coverage on television and through the other media.

    Despite these events, which formed part of the setting for our study, the public at large did not appear to have been aroused to rebellion against television for distorting its coverage of the news. As noted earlier (Table 5-1), television is rated somewhat ahead of newspapers, magazines and radio as the medium that "presents the fairest, most unbiased news," with 33 percent of the votes as compared to 23 percent for newspapers. In fact, television's relative position is improving, since ten years ago it was rated second to newspapers as the most unbiased news source.

---

    [5] Speech by Vice President Spiro Agnew in Des Moines, Iowa, at the Midwest Regional Republican Committee Meeting, November 13, 1969.

Television's score on this item, however, is neither as high a comparative rating, nor as great an improvement over 1960 as we find for other dimensions of news presentation, such as the completeness of its coverage or the speed in bringing the news. These findings are consistent with those of Harvey Jacobson, who shows in his Wisconsin study that television is farther ahead of newspapers and radio on "completeness" than on "objectivity." In commenting on his findings Jacobson makes the further point that *none* of the media is considered free of bias:

> If there are those who doubt whether a mass medium is capable of introducing bias as it mediates, the results here should give pause. If the public regarded the media as being extremely unbiased carriers of news, a mean of 1.00 would have resulted [on a rating scale running from 1 to 7]. Instead the means fell at 3.79 for radio and television, and 4.32 for newspapers.[6]

Our study does not permit an independent assessment of each of the media, but the answers to the question of which brings the "fairest, most unbiased news" are more evenly distributed among television, radio, and newspapers than are the answers to almost all the other media comparison questions, which suggests that on this count there is a harder choice for the public to make.

In the distribution of answers to this question we see a familiar pattern: the same kinds of people who *like* television better also see less bias in its news coverage (Table 5-2).

Men perceive bias somewhat more often than women, and the college educated more so than the less educated. No significant differences occur among age groups. The Republicans, along with the self-identified conservatives, are apparently a bit less likely than their opposite members to see television as the fairest of media. None of these standard groupings in our sample finds television more biased than any of the other media, such as newspapers.

Some questions added to the 1970 study permit us to pursue this question of bias, or lack of it, in television news a bit further. We asked the members of our sample whether they thought that television newscasters in general tended to color the news or tell it straight, and then what they thought of the presentation of the particular newscaster they liked most to watch. The over-all findings on the first, more general question, are seen in Table 5-3.

---

[6] Jacobson, *op. cit.*

table 5-2
"Which of the media presents the fairest, most unbiased news?"

PERCENT WHO SAY:	Television	Newspapers	Base: 100% =
Men	29	24	894
Women	37	21	974
Grade School	36	20	364
High School	36	22	1023
College	26	25	487
Democrats	35	22	939
Independents	31	20	349
Republicans	29	27	459
Liberals	35	22	548
Middle-of-the-Roaders ..	38	18	441
Conservatives	29	27	709
18–19-year olds	29	21	182
20–29	33	19	329
30–39	37	21	353
40–49	34	23	378
50–59	30	23	308
60+	34	25	414

Most of the public seems to feel it is getting its television news straight, but a sizable minority—a quarter of the sample—says that the newscasters generally color the news. People in the latter group were given a chance to expand their answers by a deliberately vague question, hopefully eliciting whatever first came to mind: "How, in what way do you think they color it?" This question might have been answered with reference

table 5-3
"Thinking of the people that give the news on TV, in general, do you feel that they let their own opinions color the way they give the news, or do they generally give the news straight, as it happened?"

	Percent
Give the news straight	54
Color the news	26
Mixed, some do, some don't	11
Don't know, can't tell	9
Base: 100 percent = 1857	

to the *political* hue of the newscasters: to the left or to the right; or it might have been answered with a description of the *technique*, or style used by the newscasters to get their own views across. All but a very few of the answers were of the latter sort, very likely because the question appeared to the respondent to call for the method of biasing rather than the direction of the bias. For instance:

> "They add onto it; they really pull it apart, like when the bomb was found in the townhouse, they made it seem bigger than it was. They don't give all the facts."

> "They usually give one-sided opinions. I think we should see two sides."

> "They let people know what they want them to know and keep from people what they don't want them to know."

> "They do it by an inflection in their voices."

> "Very biased, most of them, with facial expressions and intonations and downright distortion at times. Many times you have to get a *Christian Science Monitor* to straighten out what's been on TV."

The news *content* most frequently mentioned was the Vietnam War coverage and the treatment of large-scale civil disruption:

> "I think they hold back on important details, like how many men have been killed in Vietnam."

> "Like Vietnam, the accusations of killing over there. The newsmen should *not* express their opinions. It is no different today than World War II. We are still sending boys to war."

> "They are critical of law enforcement proceedings and are tolerant of demonstrations and riots, when only a report is necessary."

> "They overemphasize the brutality of riots by showing it over and over. That Moratorium in Washington! I turned it off. I got fed up."

As illustrated by a few of the quotes, a minority of people at least hinted at a direction in which they thought the news was tending—prorioters, or against the administration policy in Vietnam. If we very roughly classify such comments into those that imply an accusation of bias in a liberal direction (prorioters, prominority groups, antiadministration) and those that imply an accusation of conservatism, 39 respondents find a liberal bent among the newscasters and five see a conservative tendency, out of a total of 494 people who were asked the question.

With this very slim hint as to the direction of the perceived bias in mind—slim because it is based on a tiny fraction of the whole sample —one might speculate that conservatives in the population would detect bias in newscasting more than the liberals; and indeed, as we see below, the conservatives are very slightly more apt to say that "the people that give the news on TV, in general—let their own opinions color the way they give the news."

table 5-4

"Thinking of the people who report the news on TV, in general, do you feel that they let their own opinions color the way they give the news or do they report it as it happened?"

PEOPLE WHO REPORT THE NEWS ON TV

Percent Saying They:

	Conservatives	Middle-of-the-Roaders	Liberals
Give it straight	53	56	53
Color the news	30	25	26
Mixed, some color it, some don't	10	12	12
Can't tell, don't know	7	7	9
Base: 100 percent = ...	(702)	(435)	(541)

There are slightly greater (and statistically significant) differences between Democrats and Republicans. Thirty-two percent of the latter feel that the newscasters color the news, compared to 22 percent of the Democrats. Though these differences are not so pronounced as to suggest a major polarization of attitudes along political lines, they may suggest a slight tendency in that direction, with the criticism coming more from the right than from the left.

Another question that can be answered before we leave the matter of bias is this: Does the fact that 26 percent of our sample believe television colors its newscasting mean that fully a quarter of the television viewing public—a large group indeed—can find no escape from bias if they wish to watch the news on television at all? Or does television, like the printed media, offer sufficient variety to permit the individual viewer to feel he is getting the news straight from a particular newscaster chosen from among those who present the news?

table 5-5

"Is there any one newscaster you like to watch on TV more than others?"

PERCENT WHO SAY:	Total Sample	Critics	All Others
No one newscaster	27	27	27
Huntley-Brinkley	24	24	24
Walter Cronkite	25	23	26
Other network newsmen ...	4	5	2
Others (local newsmen)	20	20	20
Base: 100 percent = ...	(1779)	(466)	(1313)

"In the way the newscaster presents the news, does he give the impression of being a liberal, conservative, or middle-of-the-roader, or can't you tell?"

PERCENT WHO SAY CHOSEN NEWSCASTER APPEARS:	Total Sample	Critics	All Others
Liberal	14	21	11
Middle-of-the-roader	36	40	35
Conservative	13	14	12
Can't tell	38	25	43
Base: 100 percent = ...	(1302)	(343)	(959)

"Do you feel that (newscaster) lets his own opinions color the way he gives the news, or does he generally report it as it happened?"

PERCENT WHO SAY CHOSEN NEWSCASTER:	Total Sample	Critics	All Others
Gives it straight	78	56	86
Colors the news	6	16	2
Mixed, sometimes colored, sometimes not	11	23	7
Don't know, can't tell	5	4	5
Base: 100 percent = ...	(1308)	(344)	(964)

As a partial answer to this question, we pursued our inquiry beyond the question discussed above—newscasters in general—to a focus on one particular newscaster. Can the respondent identify one to whom he chooses to listen? What are his leanings? Does he color the news? Table 5-5 shows the answers to these questions, which were asked of both the "critics" who said that newscasters in general color the news and of those who thought the news was given straight. The critics as a group distribute their choices among newscasters precisely as do the rest of the sample: just about as many of them choose each of the big two, Walter Cronkite and Huntley–Brinkley. Chet Huntley, now retired, was still anchoring the NBC evening news in New York at the time of the interviews and was inseparable in the public mind from his Washington partner, David Brinkley. The same proportion of both groups choose from among several other network newsmen, none of whom received more than one percent of the total choices, and from among an even wider scattering of newscasters affiliated with local broadcasting stations around the country. Also, precisely equal proportions of critics and others choose *some* newscaster to watch, which would suggest that the critics feel no more left out in the cold than the noncritics; of course, the critical group may possibly consider it more of a choice among evils.

We also see in the answers to the second question that the critics are not much better than the others in detecting an ideological leaning—toward liberalism or toward conservatism—on the part of the chosen newsman. When rated by critics, impressions of newscasters in the "middle-of-the-road" and the "can't tell" categories *combined* outnumber the impressions that the newscaster is either liberal or conservative. While the critics do find both liberalism and conservatism to a greater degree (more of the latter than the former), none of these differences are statistically significant.

In answers to the third question, we find a small hard-core critical group, composed of 16 percent of the critics (or about 4 percent of the *total* sample), who not only see the news in general as being biased, but who even believe their own chosen newscasters color the news. Most of the other critics tell us, in regard to the newscaster they like to watch the most, that he gives the news straight or that they cannot tell whether he is coloring the news or not. So it appears that there are very few people who feel that they cannot watch the news on television without exposing themselves to biased presentations.

A look at one more set of data may help to cast further light on these findings. Is it possible that the lack of bias seen in the selected newscaster results from a tendency of people to choose newscasters who conform to their own political self-identifications? Do the people who identify themselves as "liberal" tend to pick newscasters who give the impression of being liberal in presenting the news? Do conservatives consciously pick conservative-sounding newscasters?

The conservatives in the sample do tend to choose conservative-sounding newscasters somewhat more than is the case among liberals or middle-of-the-roaders. On the other hand, it is the self-identified middle-of-the-roaders rather than the liberals who tend to choose the liberal-

table 5-6

"In the way (particular newscaster watched most often) presents the news, does he give the impression of being a liberal, conservative, middle-of-the-roader, or can't you tell?"

	Liberals	Middle-Roaders	Conserva-tives	All
PERCENT WHO SAY CHOSEN NEWSCASTER APPEARS:				
Liberal	8	28	11	13
Conservative	9	6	21	14
Middle-of-the-roader and				
Can't tell	83	66	69	74
Base: 100 percent = ...	(381)	(308)	(520)	(1209)

appearing newscasters. But the majority of people in each group do not detect any bias in the way in which their newscasters present the news. The findings are not sufficiently consistent to prove the case for a wide-spread tendency of people to select the news presentations that fit their predilections. Most of them either don't find the congenial bias, or if they do, they don't perceive it as bias.

In summary, it appears that a sizeable proportion (about one-fourth) of the public feels that television news is generally biased in its presenta-tion. A much smaller group of hard-core critics think even their *own* favorite newscaster colors the news. But the vast majority of people either accept the objectivity of television newscasting in general or find a spe-cific newscaster to watch who is felt to be objective in his reporting. It is far beyond the scope of this study to determine the actual extent of bias in television journalism; we can only report popular views on the question. If the public at large were the judge, the medium would probably be exonerated or at worst be given a suspended sentence.

GOOD NEWS AND BAD NEWS

Does television in its day-to-day coverage of events and in its news docu-mentaries pay too much attention to the socially disruptive, to aberrant radicalism, to the unpleasant and disturbing aspects of national life? Is it fair to neglect the more normal—the students who are not protesting, the peaceful cities, and the well-fed populace? These are eminently debatable questions—questions which were given a considerable amount of public attention and discussion at the time that the field interviews were carried out. We let our sample of the American public in on the debate at several points in the course of the interviews—initially when they were asked to evaluate the media comparatively, and in later questions about news of a disconcerting nature.

We are confronted with some interesting findings from two parallel questions concerning the nature of television's emphasis on the good and the bad in comparison with newspapers, radio, and magazines (Chart 5-1).

chart 5-1

"Now, I would like to get your opinions about how radio, newspapers, television, and magazines compare. Generally speaking, which of these puts the most emphasis on the bad things going on in America?"

"And which puts the most emphasis on the good things going on in America?"

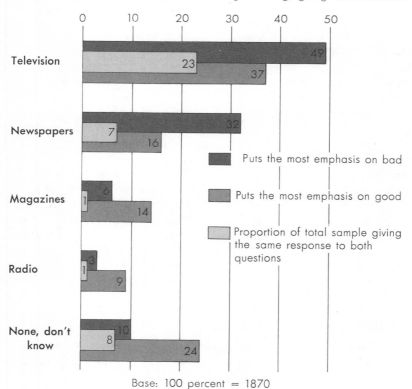

Base: 100 percent = 1870

In response to both of the questions, emphasis on "bad" news and emphasis on "good" news, television receives a plurality of the choices. There were more people, 49 percent to 37 percent, who saw television as the bearer of bad rather than of good tidings, but there was also a considerable number—23 percent of the entire sample—who answered "television" to *both* questions—saying it emphasizes *both* the good and the bad. One might suspect here a "response set"—a tendency for people without thinking about it to say "television" in answer to almost any question in an interview dealing with television. These questions, however, were asked at the beginning of the interview before the central theme of the inquiry became evident, so an alternative interpretation might be suggested: that for a large group of viewers television is simply so dominant a medium in bringing all the news, any sort of news, that they see it as emphasizing all things—both the good and the bad—without any sense of contradiction. Yes, it emphasizes the good things, yes it emphasizes the bad things; it emphasizes everything.

table 5-7
Profile of Those Who Think Television Emphasizes Bad Things

"Which (of the four media) puts the most emphasis on the bad things going on in America?"

PERCENT SAYING:	Television	Base: 100% =
Male	51	890
Female	47	974
Grade School	50	365
High School	49	1020
College	47	485
18–29-year olds	40	419
30–49	53	728
50+	51	722
Liberals	50	544
Middle-of-the-roaders	50	439
Conservatives	52	708
Heavy Viewers	50	634
Moderate Viewers	51	646
Light Viewers	46	602

Those who see television as the bearer of bad tidings display a rather flat profile (Table 5-7). They are fairly evenly divided between men and women, heavy and light viewers of television, liberals and conservatives and between the higher educated and the lower. It would appear to be a hard group to characterize sociologically, except in the one variable of age. A significantly larger proportion of the thirty-and-over viewers than of the under thirty's see television as the medium that emphasizes the bad. This is a finding worth pursuing, since there are relatively few points in our inquiry where we find age making much of a difference (for example, in comparison with education) in its effects on attitudes toward the medium and its content.

Further evidence that the young viewers may sometimes feel quite differently from the older is found in answers to two questions dealing with specific types of events covered by news programs in the period preceding the study, in that era of street riots, student rebellions, and political assassinations. During the first nine months of 1967 the Kerner Commission identified 41 "major" or "serious" racial disorders in American cities;[7] the spring and summer of 1968 brought another round of urban riots, following the assassination of Martin Luther King. Starting at Berkeley in 1964 and culminating at Kent State and Jackson State in 1970, student protests disrupted college and university campuses in all parts of the country. Off-campus antiwar demonstrations occurred intermittently between the March-on-the-Pentagon in 1967 and Mobilization Day in 1969. The news was "bad" in the late sixties and becoming worse during a period when television was expanding and improving the technical quality of its news coverage—and at the same time that more and more people were relying on television as their chief source of news.

The first of our two questions whose responses are shown in Table 5-8, asked about programs that deal with social problems—race relations and campus unrest—are there too many or too few such programs?

Youth's relative receptivity to the problem-oriented national news of the 1960s stands out in these tabulations. Only 12 percent of the teenagers seem to mind all those programs about campus unrest and a large proportion of them (45 percent) feels that there are not enough of such programs. In the sixty-and-over group, the sentiments are reversed, with 45 percent saying "too many" and 16 percent saying "not enough." In the reactions to this question, the amount of education would appear to make some difference too, and the data do show that those with college education are slightly more receptive to social-problem programming than

---

[7] National Advisory Commission on Civil Disorders, *Report*, Washington, D.C., March 1, 1968.

table 5-8

"Television programs can be designed to provide different things. From your point of view, does television today have enough, not enough, or too many of each of these kinds of program?

"Programs that provide information about social problems in the U.S., like racial problems and problems on college campuses?"

PERCENT SAYING:	Not Enough	Enough	Too Many	Base: 100% =
Male	28	37	35	721
Female	26	45	30	759
Grade School	16	47	37	226
High School	26	42	33	828
College	34	36	30	433
18–19-year olds	48	40	12	156
20–29	40	43	17	276
30–39	44	37	19	293
40–49	23	44	33	307
50–59	18	35	47	228
60+	16	39	45	304
Democrats	28	39	33	715
Independents	25	44	31	297
Republicans	24	43	33	377
Liberals	26	44	31	420
Middle-of-the-roaders	36	39	25	359
Conservatives	23	40	37	583
Heavy Viewers	26	43	30	519
Moderate Viewers	24	42	33	534
Light Viewers	30	36	33	402
Total	27	41	32	1486

are their fellow viewers with less education. Education and age are inter-related characteristics in the U.S. population; the young are apt to have more schooling than the old—so the findings are not surprising.

A more complete picture emerges by treating the two charac-teristics—age and amount of education—simultaneously, as has been done in Charts 5-2 and 5-3. It is, indeed, age that makes the difference in re-

chart 5-2

Responses by Age and Education of Respondents

"From your point of view, does television today have enough, not enough, or too many programs that provide information about social problems in the U.S., like racial problems and problems on college campuses?"

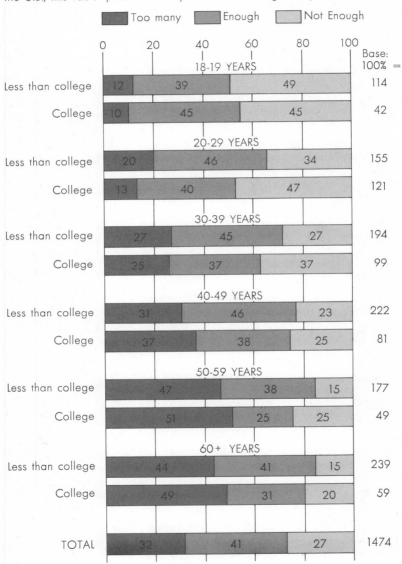

	Too many	Enough	Not Enough	Base: 100% =
18-19 YEARS				
Less than college	12	39	49	114
College	10	45	45	42
20-29 YEARS				
Less than college	20	46	34	155
College	13	40	47	121
30-39 YEARS				
Less than college	27	45	27	194
College	25	37	37	99
40-49 YEARS				
Less than college	31	46	23	222
College	37	38	25	81
50-59 YEARS				
Less than college	47	38	15	177
College	51	25	25	49
60+ YEARS				
Less than college	44	41	15	239
College	49	31	20	59
TOTAL	32	41	27	1474

chart 5-3

Responses by Age and Education of Respondents

"As far as your own viewing is concerned, is this a change for the better, a change for the worse, or hasn't it made any difference to you: more live coverage of disruptions in the U.S., such as riots and protests in the streets?"

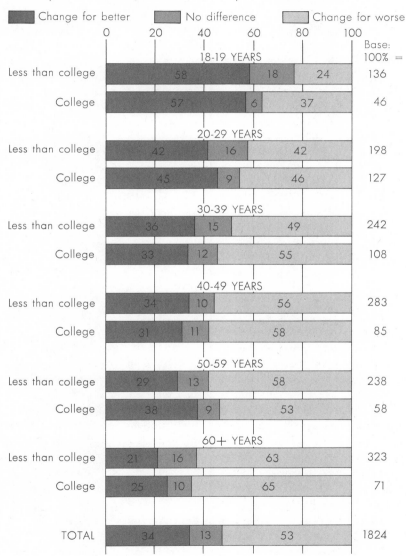

actions to news about social problems. Among the young, regardless of education, there are many more who think there are too few programs about race and campus unrest than think there are too many, and there are many more who find coverage of street protests a change for the better than find it a change for the worse. On both scores, the opposite is true for the older viewers, regardless of education.

The answers to these questions show a much closer relationship to age than do the responses to any other questions in the entire study. The young and the old do not differ very much in their attitudes toward television as a medium, or in their views as to its effect on children, or in their evaluations of most of the changes that have taken place in the medium. If anything, the older viewers are a bit more pro-TV on most topics. The significant difference between the old and the young is in their reactions to the presentation of news about social problems and social disruption. It is evident that we are observing here a reaction to the content of the news rather than to the medium of its transmission. The young have been shown in other studies, such as those conducted for the Kerner Commission, to be more tolerant than the old of the actuality of social ferment and of the violence that may occur in protest movements.[8] The happenings themselves do not seem so bad to the young, and the news about the happenings is quite tolerable, even welcomed. The old, it appears, don't like it and don't want to hear about it.

A SPEEDY MESSENGER?

A majority of people in our sample *think* that television is the speediest medium in bringing the latest news, a public perception that has been found in other studies.[9] But this is not always true, according to the results of communication studies designed to assess the relative speed of various media of communication by focusing on important events and inquiring as to the means by which people first heard about them. Public opinion studies immediately following the shooting and death of President John Kennedy showed that the news spread extremely rapidly but not primarily by means of television. In San Jose, California, half of those who heard the news early first heard it from other people, and only 22 percent heard it on television (27 percent on radio); and in Iowa City 55 percent heard the news first through others, 25 percent by radio and 19 percent on

---

[8] National Advisory Commission on Civil Disorders.
[9] Leo Bogart, *The Age of Television*, p. 369.

television.[10] Following the more recent tragedy affecting the Kennedy family, the assassination of Senator Robert Kennedy, a national telephone survey found that 57 percent of the persons interviewed first heard of the shooting on the radio.[11]

An accident of timing allowed us to examine this apparent discrepancy between how people *think* they get the news most quickly, and how they may *actually* find out about a particular dramatic event. The interviewing of our special sample in Minneapolis–St. Paul started on April 12, 1970. During the evening of the thirteenth, the Apollo 13 mission, two days into its journey to the moon, developed the power failure which destroyed its chances for a moon landing and placed the lives of the three astronauts aboard in jeopardy. The news of the trouble was first broadcast on one regular network news program in Minneapolis–St. Paul at 10:20 P.M., and was quickly picked up by the other networks and the independent stations, interrupting some programs with news flashes, pre-empting others during the remainder of the evening. It was certainly one of the biggest news events of 1970. We had already planned to ask our interviewees the general media comparison question, "Which would you say brings you the latest news most quickly?," and as a result of this news event we were able to add some questions about the Apollo 13 flight.

The Minneapolis–St. Paul answers to the general question were roughly similar to the national sample's answers as shown in Table 5-9.

table 5-9

"Which [among the media] brings you the latest news most quickly?"

PERCENT SAYING:	Minneapolis–St. Paul	National Sample
Television	52	55
Radio	46	39
Newspapers	3	6
Magazines	0	0
Base: 100 percent =	(338)	(1888)

Again we find television's popular reputation as the speediest messenger surpassing radio's. But television did not quite live up to its

---

[10] Bradley S. Greenburg, "Diffusion of News of the Kennedy Assassination," *Public Opinion Quarterly*, XXVIII–ii (1964), pp. 225–232.
[11] Leo Bogart, *The Age of Television*, p. 440.

reputation when it came to bringing the news about Apollo 13's flight. Table 5-10 shows how the whole Minneapolis–St. Paul sample answered the Apollo 13 question and how it was answered by those who had said a moment before that television generally "brings them the latest news most quickly."

Now we find, in line with the studies mentioned above, that television appears not to be the quickest when people are queried about the particular event rather than the general rule. Radio, in Minneapolis–St. Paul, brought the first word about trouble on the Apollo flight to more people, by 58 percent to 40 percent. Television did, as expected, bring the first word to a higher proportion of those who thought it speediest among the media. But even among that group, nearly half first got news of this one event by some other means.

Some light may be thrown on the apparent discrepancy by seeing, in sequence, the answers to three questions—the general and the specific ones shown in Table 5-10 and a subsequent question—in which we asked about sources of information regarding Apollo 13 following the initial discovery (Chart 5-4). The sample is split so that we can examine the answers on the three questions of the men and women separately, the latter being known for the longer hours they are apt to spend in the presence of the set.

Men differ markedly between the *general* rule, where they split evenly between radio and television as the quickest conveyor of news, and the *particular case*, where radio appears far quicker. Forty-eight percent of the men see television as generally the speediest medium, a figure that decreases to 25 percent, for news via television, when queried about

table 5-10

"How did you first find out that something had gone wrong on the Apollo 13 flight? Was it from newspapers, radio, TV or from other persons?"

PERCENT SAYING:*	Total	Those Who Think Television Quickest	Those Who Think Other Media Quickest
Television	40	53	26
Radio	58	45	71
Newspapers	2	1	4
Base: 100 percent =	(274)	(138)	(136)

* Excludes those who mentioned "other persons" as a source.

chart 5-4
Television as a Quick Source of News

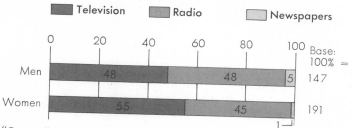

"Generally speaking, which brings you the latest news most quickly?"

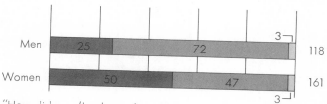

"How did you *first* learn that something had gone wrong on Apollo 13?"

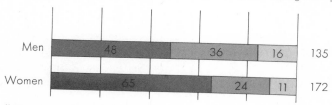

"After that, where did you get most of your information
about what was happening to Apollo 13?"

first finding out about Apollo 13. The women are much more consistent, but even for them there is a decrease in the proportion for whom television was the first source of Apollo 13 news: 55 percent of the women say television is generally the quickest medium, while 50 percent heard the Apollo news on it, of those who mentioned any news medium as the source.

The Apollo flight lasted for another four days until its safe return to the Pacific Ocean on April 17. During that period of tension and uncertainty about the fate of the flight crew, television re-emerged as the predominant source of information, with 48 percent of the men and 65 percent of the women saying that they got most of their "information about what was happening to the Apollo 13 flight" via television. Radio remained the chief source for about a third of the men and 24 percent of the women; newspapers played much less of a role.

A pattern emerges from these findings when seen in sequence. Television is perceived as the medium that brings the news most quickly, and for an increasing proportion of the population—probably a majority —it is the first source of information about most events in the news. In the case of highly dramatic events, however, such as trouble in space or a political assassination, the news first reaches most people by other means, by radio or by other people telling them about it. Then, as the story unfolds, people return to the television set for further news.

This shifting away and returning to the fold is a trait characteristic of men more than of women, according to the Minneapolis findings. Unfortunately we do not know what the men and women were doing from 10:20 P.M. on, on April 13, or how many of the women snapped on the TV set first thing the next morning and got the news as their husbands went off to work to hear about it on the car radio or from fellow-workers. An accident of time—an event happening at night—might have created an unusual set of communications circumstances. But it is likely that similar patterns could have occurred with almost any other timing of events.

ELECTION COVERAGE AND ITS EFFECTS

This study did not attempt to assess popular reaction to political advertising, which constitutes a large part of the total political fare that appears on the screen—programs and spot announcements bought by candidates and their parties at election time. But we did ask people for their reactions to network and broadcasting stations' own coverage of politics. It is unlikely that these two aspects of political coverage are easily separable in the minds of the viewers, especially when so much of political advertising on television has adopted the formats previously associated with television journalism, such as the single reporter interview, the staged press conference, the topical panel discussion and the use of excerpts taken from speeches previously covered by the news cameramen. In examining our data, we must assume that people's attitudes on political coverage by television *may* reflect their viewing both of the coverage given by broadcasting news departments and of the products of campaign managers who purchase television time.

That television reaches huge audiences in its political broadcasting is quite evident. For example, each of the Nixon–Kennedy debates in 1960 was seen by at least 60 million viewers. Over 90 million adults of voting age watched some part of the proceedings at the Democratic convention on Wednesday night, August 28, 1968 and over 61 million saw the balloting on Humphrey's nomination. The connection between exposure and effect, for instance, the effect of watching political broadcasts on people's decisions whether or not to vote for one candidate rather than another, is far more difficult to establish, despite a substantial body of research on the subject. Most of the research tends to confirm long-established communication principles. The amount of new information that any mass medium can impart to the public is limited by the fact that it is the already better informed members of the public who tend to seek new information. Added to this is a tendency for people to use communications selectively in accordance with established predispositions, tuning in when the ideas expressed are congenial and tuning out when they are not. And even when people do expose themselves to the message, a degree of "selective perception" may operate, permitting two people to see the same content and receive different impressions from it, each in accordance with what he wants to believe.[12]

The prevalence of such phenomena militates against facile assumptions of a direct connection between political communications which are calculated to persuade, and their ability to do so. Most researchers conclude that the major effect is in the reinforcement of existing attitudes rather than in the conversion to new ones. Beyond this, there is some evidence from other research that television, with its huge audience, has not even heightened interest in politics to the point of significantly increasing participation in national elections. Angus Campbell, in an examination of voting turnout figures—the proportion of adults who voted in presidential and congressional elections—shows only a very modest increase in turnout for presidential elections during the era of television's dramatic expansion, and no increase at all for congressional elections. This he compares with the pretelevision era, where he finds a sharp increase in turnout as radio penetrated into more and more homes. Survey findings reported by Campbell also show little correspondence between the amount of television coverage given to campaigns between 1952 and 1960, and the amount of interest people expressed in the campaigns or in the outcome of the elections.[13] Restricting as such findings may be to the assumption of a direct and powerful political influence exerted by the medium, the extent of television's political effectiveness remains a subject of debate, with some students of communication still insisting on television's ability to alter

---

[12] Joseph Klapper, *The Effects of Mass Communication*, Glencoe, Illinois: Free Press, 1961.

[13] Angus Campbell, "Has Television Reshaped Politics," in E.C. Dreyer and W.A. Rosenbaum, eds., *Political Opinion and Electoral Behavior*, Belmont, California: Wadsworth Publishing Co., 1966; and William Glaser, "Television and Voter Turnout," *Public Opinion Quarterly*, Spring 1965, pp. 71–87.

public attitudes and values almost instantaneously;[14] others suggest that if the effect of the medium in the political sphere is not immediate and direct, it may still be there, indirectly and slowly shaping the public's political attitudes and actions.[15]

Most would agree that political personalities become known to vast numbers of potential voters simply because television reaches so many households so constantly. Furthermore, television and radio reach not only a larger, but also a differently constituted audience than do the printed media. The more affluent and better-educated members of the public are apt as a matter of habit to read newspapers and news magazines considerably more than the poorer and less well educated; this is not the case in television viewing, which is spread fairly evenly among economic and educational groups. The *potential* of television to involve those parts of the electorate that have been traditionally less involved in politics and less inclined to exercise the franchise is evident. Some recent research has suggested that with television there may be a break in the dam that has kept the less informed and involved always less likely to become informed or involved. Jay Blumler, in detailed studies of television's political role in English elections (with findings applicable to the United States) concludes that in the 1964 general election "the average amount of information that had been gained [through television] during the campaign, by those individuals whose motivation was weak, was not appreciably less than the average gain recorded in the top group" (that is, the group with the highest political motivation).[16]

Some data in our study bear peripherally on these questions. No attempt was made to trace the political activities of our respondents directly to views about television, but we do have information about the political affiliations of the sample members and their leanings toward liberalism or conservatism as well as the standard background information. They were also asked a series of questions about their attitudes toward political coverage on television and their own assessment of the effects that television treatment of the 1968 campaign may have had on their decisions.

Between 1960 and 1970 television took a significant leap in the public's view as the medium giving the "clearest understanding" of national elections. At the beginning of the decade it received 42 percent of the choices among the four media, with newspapers receiving 36 percent. In

---

[14] Marshall McLuhan, *Understanding Media: The Extensions of Man*, New York: McGraw-Hill Book Company, 1964.

[15] Harold Mendelsohn and Irving Crespi, *Polls, Television and the New Politics*, Scranton, Pennsylvania: Chandler Publishing Company, 1970.

[16] Jay G. Blumler and Denis McQuail, *Television in Politics*, Chicago: University of Chicago Press, 1969.

1970, 59 percent of the public chose television to 21 percent for newspapers. The group composition of those who chose television in 1970 as the medium giving the clearest picture is shown in Table 5-11.

table 5-11

"Which [of the media] gives you the clearest understanding of the candidates and issues in national elections?"

PERCENT SAYING:	Television	Base: 100% =
Male	55	895
Female	63	976
Grade School	64	366
High School	60	1024
College	51	486
18–29-Year Olds	61	421
30–49-Year Olds	58	733
50+-Year Olds	58	721
Blue Collar	64	870
White Collar	52	669
Democrats	63	933
Independents	54	345
Republicans	56	457
Liberals	62	547
Middle-of-the-Roaders	57	440
Conservatives	60	710
Heavy Viewers	67	635
Moderate Viewers	58	652
Light Viewers	53	601

The choices for television over the other media are proportionately higher among the less well educated, among the blue collar workers and among Democrats. Since education, occupation, and party preference are associated variables, these findings are consistent with one another and are hardly unexpected. Similarly more heavy than light television viewers and more women than men find "the clearest understanding" of elections on television. None of the differences are very pronounced.

In order to re-examine these general tendencies in a more specific context, three questions were asked in the 1970 study about television coverage of the most recent presidential election. The 1968 campaign had culminated in Nixon's victory about sixteen months before our interviewing. How good a job, we asked, did television do in covering the campaign? Did TV coverage affect people's views about the candidates? Should there be more of it in the future? The answers of the total sample to these questions are shown in Table 5-12.

table 5-12

"Thinking back to the presidential election of 1968 for a moment—the one in which Hubert Humphrey, George Wallace, and Richard Nixon were candidates—In your opinion, did television do an excellent, good, only fair, or poor job in presenting the issues and candidates to the public?"

	Percent
Excellent	13
Good	44
Only fair	25
Poor	8
Don't know	10

Base: 100 percent = 1856

"As compared to what was done in 1968, do you think television should present more programs about the candidates and issues that will be coming up in the 1972 presidential election, fewer programs, or about the same number of programs?"

	Percent
More	32
Fewer	15
About the same	48
Don't know	6

Base: 100 percent = 1853

"Did TV play a very important part, a fairly important part, or no part at all in helping you to decide whom you wanted to win in the election of 1968?"

	Percent
Very important	13
Fairly important	30
No part	53
Don't know	4

Base: 100 percent = 1848

As the data show, television received a fairly high rating on its performance in 1968 (57 percent saying "good" or "excellent," almost the same proportion of the public that finds television superior to the other media in bringing "understanding" about campaigns). In answers to the second question, the largest group wants about the same amount of campaign coverage the next time around; of those who want change, twice as many want more programs as want fewer.

The answers to these two questions may be given a reasonable amount of credence; they are consistent with other public assessments of television as a communicator of political information. However, the question about TV's influence on preferences among candidates elicited responses that are both more surprising and more susceptible to over-interpretation. According to the survey, 43 percent of the public seems to say that television coverage led to some choice of candidate that would not have occurred without it—a remarkable effect if true. But it is most unlikely that television, by itself, sent many Democrats fleeing into the Nixon camp or created many Humphrey fans out of Wallacites. The party affiliations of most of the sample were already established; the candidates were well known before the campaign started, and influences other than that of television were at work. It is more reasonable to interpret the high figure for perceived influence as reflecting a sense of increased familiarity with the candidates and, most likely, a reinforcement of pre-existing tendencies.

With that caveat in mind, we may examine in Chart 5-5 the sub-group composition of the answers to the question, remembering we are looking only at a perception of political influence which may or may not have been translated into altered decisions in the voting booth.

Only two variables among the ones shown here appear to make any difference at all in perceptions of television's influences. Women see coverage of the 1968 campaign as having played slightly more of a part in their decisions about candidates than men, and younger people detect a bit more influence than the older. These small differences are of no particular significance by themselves, but they are interesting in relationship to the answers to the previous question about political coverage in 1972, which are shown in Table 5-13.

The women in the sample, while feeling TV's political influence more, are less desirous than men of extensive coverage—a hint of a stereo-typed sex role, the persuadable, but essentially nonpolitical female. Or it may be that the women have simply seen too much of politics on their television sets.

The difference between the age groups, with 47 percent of the young and 34 percent of the 50-and-overs perceiving some influence in

125

chart 5-5

"Did T.V. play a very important part, a fairly important part, or no part at all in helping you to decide whom you wanted to win the election in 1968?"

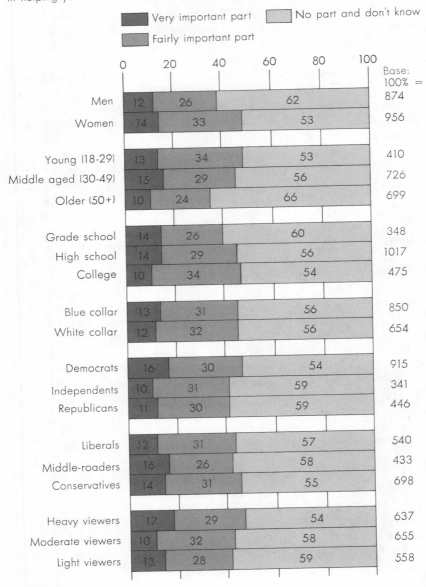

	Very important part	Fairly important part	No part and don't know	Base: 100% =
Men	12	26	62	874
Women	14	33	53	956
Young (18-29)	13	34	53	410
Middle aged (30-49)	15	29	56	726
Older (50+)	10	24	66	699
Grade school	14	26	60	348
High school	14	29	56	1017
College	10	34	54	475
Blue collar	13	31	56	850
White collar	12	32	56	654
Democrats	16	30	54	915
Independents	10	31	59	341
Republicans	11	30	59	446
Liberals	12	31	57	540
Middle-roaders	16	26	58	433
Conservatives	14	31	55	698
Heavy viewers	17	29	54	637
Moderate viewers	10	32	58	655
Light viewers	13	28	59	558

table 5-13

"As compared to what was done in 1968, do you think television should present more programs about the candidates and issues in the 1972 presidential election, fewer programs, or about the same number of programs?"

Percent Asking for "More" Political Coverage in 1972

	Percent	Base: 100% =
SEX:		
Men	36	876
Women	27	959
AGE:		
18–29	37	416
30–49	32	724
50+	29	699

1968 (Chart 5-5) and also with more of the young than of the old wanting more coverage in the future (Table 5-13), fits another cultural stereotype —that of the older person with established political views and habits, less likely to be influenced by the campaign and less interested in having more political fare on the air. It is interesting to note that the two groups that perceive more influence of television than others are traditionally less likely to participate in elections. The young turn out on election day less frequently than the old, and women, though they have been catching up with men in the exercise of their franchise in recent years, still tend to lag behind in most elections.[17]

In respect to all the other variables shown, the variations are remarkably small; there are practically no differences between educational and occupational groups, between liberals and conservatives, Democrats and Republicans, or heavy and light viewers of television. It appears to be an uninteresting set of findings unless one entertains hypotheses about differences that should occur. Should the less educated, more dependent than others on TV for their news, feel themselves more susceptible to the persuasive influences of its campaign coverage? Should not the self-

---

[17] U. S. Department of Commerce, Bureau of the Census *Population Characteristics: Voting and Registration in the Election of November 1968*, P–20, No. 192, December 2, 1969, Table I, p. 10.

proclaimed political "independents" be more susceptible to influence than the presumably more committed Democrats and Republicans? The indications, from answers to this one question, are that television does not tend to favor one faction over another in such a way as to suggest a partisan political influence during a campaign, or even to discriminate among the social groups of which the population is composed. To an amazing degree the perceived effects of television's political coverage are spread evenly among the public.

The high assessment of television in its journalistic role that has been shown in this chapter certainly represents a general public endorsement, all the more resounding since it occurs at a time when TV news is under attack.

Clearly, this part of television's content has largely been exempted from the trend toward a lower public esteem for the medium as a whole. But the vote is by no means unanimous. TV news presentation is not free of the suspicion of bias that the American public accords to all the mass media; and while the improvements in the technology of rapid worldwide coverage of daily events may be roundly applauded, there are those who would prefer less emphasis on the unpleasant and disturbing national conflicts.

CHAPTER 6

WHAT THEY SAY AND WHAT THEY SEE IN MINNEAPOLIS–ST. PAUL

In 1960 Gary Steiner compared what people said they liked about television with what they actually watched by interviewing a sample of New Yorkers who had previously kept viewing diaries for the American Research Bureau, a leading national TV rating service. We followed the same procedure in 1970, again with the cooperation of ARB, but this time in Minneapolis–St. Paul, a city chosen somewhat arbitrarily. Its main virtue for our purpose was that it offered a fairly representative mix of broadcasting stations—three network affiliates, an independent VHF station, a VHF educational channel, and two UHF stations.

Each person interviewed in the sample of 344 cases had completed a diary on a week's television viewing during the month of November 1969; they were contacted again some five months later as part of the national study, and were asked many but not all of the questions we asked of the cross-sectional sample. After tabulating the programs broadcast in the city during the diary-keeping weeks, we then had three sources of data to examine and compare: the actual program offerings in Minneapolis–St. Paul during the month of November (the Menu), the diary records of programs watched (the Diet), and the characteristics and attitudes of the viewers as reported to the interviewers. In the following pages we can see how people's diet compares with the menu, how their characteristics affect what they watch, and how what they say they want on television relates to what they actually view.

MENU AND DIET

The menu of television fare during those November weeks included all the weekday evenings (5:00 P.M. to sign off) and weekend programs carried by the five local VHF stations; each of which could be reached with a good picture on the sets in the interviewed households. Our interviews revealed that the other two broadcasting stations in Minneapolis–St. Paul could not be received well enough to warrant inclusion in the study. Seventy-five percent of the respondents said that they could not get one of the UHF stations, at all; only 13 percent could get it with a "good picture." No one in the sample could receive the second UHF station.

The programs were classified according to the eleven program types which Steiner had established for the 1960 study: *comedy-variety, movies, action, sports, light music, heavy music, light drama, heavy drama, information,* and *public affairs, news* and *religion.* We used unduplicated minutes of programming as the measure; for example, three simultaneous half-hour news programs on three different channels were counted as 30 minutes rather than 90 minutes of news programming. In Steiner's study, the measure used was the number of *programs* in a category.

There is a reasonably close correspondence between the amount of time the broadcasting stations allocated to programs of various types and the time people spent viewing them. Table 6-1 shows some notable exceptions. Entertainment programming is a bit overconsumed: the average proportion of people's time spent watching is greater than the share of unduplicated minutes given to entertainment shows by the stations. Steiner found a similar correspondence between programs available and programs watched in the entertainment areas, except in the case of movies where there were almost three times as many programs as viewers. The latter discrepancy would not have been as great if Steiner had used the measure of unduplicated minutes of programming rather than the number of programs, since movies tended to appear simultaneously late at night in that era. This menu-diet difference was reduced by the time of the 1970 study because of a programming change by commercial stations, shifting some of the movies from late-night to the early evening hours when the audience is larger.

The largest discrepancies in 1970 appear in the news and information categories. There was a considerable overconsumption of news; 9 percent of the unduplicated minutes of broadcasting time was devoted to

table 6-1
The Diet versus the Menu Minneapolis 1970 Program Composition (expressed in percentages of total minutes of TV watched and available by program type)

PROGRAM TYPE	Unduplicated Minutes Available	Minutes Watched
Comedy-variety	21	26
Movies	18	20
Action	14	16
Sports	9	9
Light music	5	10
Light drama	1	2
News	9	15
Information and public affairs	16	2
Heavy drama	3	—
Religion	2	—
Heavy music	1	—
N(number of viewers) = 344		
Base: 100 percent =	42,675	317,965

news, while 15 percent of the viewers' time was spent watching it. Since news programs tend to appear simultaneously in the evening, the menu figure is smaller than in some other types of programming where fewer of the programs are duplicated by others in the same category. However, that is probably only a partial explanation of the discrepancy. Steiner found the same phenomenon in 1960 using the number of programs in a category, whether duplicated or not: the proportion of news programs viewed was higher than the proportion of programs available. We must assume that news programs of 1970 were extremely popular and that they appeared at times when larger audiences were available to watch them. Information and public affairs programs, on the other hand, suffered from audience neglect as they had in New York in 1960; Steiner noted, then, that the disproportionately large number of the programs receiving small audiences "must have a great deal to do with their concentration in hours that are often unattended"—that is, during Saturday or Sunday afternoons when audiences are low, rather than on weekday or weekend evenings. The same explanation cannot apply in Minneapolis–St. Paul in 1970; a good proportion of the information and public affairs programs then appeared in prime time, some on the commercial channels, and many more on the educational television station. If we had limited our account of the menu to the commercial channels, some of this discrepancy between menu and diet might have disappeared. The survey found, nevertheless, that the Minneapolan is not taking advantage of what is available on his VHF dial —a finding which applies, as we will soon see, even to those groups that request more informational shows on television. As a final note on this table, heavy drama, classical music, and religious programs did not reach enough of the audience to be recorded as part of the viewer's diet.

DIET AND THE CHARACTERISTICS OF VIEWERS

When we compare the viewing of people with different background characteristics (level of education, men and women, various ages) we find remarkable similarity, despite the fact that they often express different

table 6-2

Diet by Education (expressed in percentages of total minutes of TV watched by program type)

PROGRAM TYPE	EDUCATION			
	0–8 yrs.	9–11 yrs.	12 yrs.	1–4 yrs. College
Comedy-variety	27	25	27	23
Movies	16	19	21	20
Action	17	17	16	15
Sports	6	9	8	13
Light music	11	11	10	8
Light drama	1	2	3	2
News	20	15	14	17
Information and public affairs	2	2	2	2
Heavy drama	—	—	—	1
Religion	1	1	—	—
Heavy music	—	—	—	—
Base (Minutes): 100 percent =	41,535	39,540	163,150	73,740
N (number of viewers) =	(38)	(38)	(176)	(76)

attitudes toward the medium. This is a repetition of a Steiner finding ten years earlier, but now the differences between the groups are even smaller. Tables 6-2 through 6-4 show the 1970 findings.

The college graduate and the viewer with just a grammar school education spend almost precisely the same proportion of their viewing time watching entertainment programs; more sports and movies for the former and a bit more action and comedy programs for the latter, but hardly a distinct segmentation of the audience by educational groups. The small audience for information programs is distributed evenly among all educational categories while the popular regular news programs take up slightly more of the viewing time of the lowest educational group.

In Table 6-3 we see a similar lack of differentiation by age of the viewers, where only two differences are even worth noting. Older people spend more of their time watching the news programs and the not so old (under 55) tend to watch more movies. And again between the two sexes,

table 6-3
Diet by Age (expressed in percentages of total minutes of TV watched by program type)

PROGRAM TYPE	AGE		
	Under 35 yrs.	35–54 yrs.	55 yrs. and Over
Comedy-variety	28	23	27
Movies	21	24	13
Action	17	16	16
Sports	9	10	8
Light music	9	8	12
Light drama	3	2	2
News	11	16	19
Information and public affairs	2	2	3
Heavy drama	—	—	—
Religion	—	—	1
Heavy music	—	—	—
Base (Minutes): 100 percent = ...	98,025	124,365	95,575
N (number of viewers) = ...	(113)	(149)	(82)

table 6-4

Diet by Sex (expressed in percentages of total minutes of TV watched by program type)

	SEX	
PROGRAM TYPE	Male	Female
Comedy-variety	22	28
Movies	21	19
Action	16	16
Sports	13	6
Light music	8	10
Light drama	2	3
News	15	15
Information and public affairs	2	2
Heavy drama	—	—
Religion	—	—
Heavy music	—	—
Base (Minutes): 100 percent = ...126,030	126,030	191,940
N (number of viewers) = ...	151	193

the differences are minor (Table 6-4). The men, as expected, spend more time with sports (football was in mid-season in November) and the women watch more comedy and variety shows. We might have expected, with many more multiset households in 1970, that husbands and wives could go their separate TV ways to a greater extent, but apparently they have not chosen to do so.

VIEWING AND ATTITUDES

In discussing his 1960 findings, Steiner pointed to a lack of consistency between what different groups of respondents said they wanted television to provide, and what they actually watched. Steiner notes, for instance, that the expressed desire for more information programming did not increase with the age of the respondents, but the *viewing* of information and news programs did. The better educated, on the other hand, said they wanted more information, but their viewing of it was about the same as that of the less-educated groups. It is this relationship—or lack of it—

between expressed views and patterns of actual viewing that we will now examine with the Minneapolis–St. Paul sample, comparing what the respondents say about television with their diary records of a week's viewing.

To begin with, generalized attitudes toward television appear not to affect patterns of viewing at all (Table 6-5). Using a rigorous criterion of the TV fan—a very high score on the battery of attitude items—we see he has only a slight tendency to watch less news and more of other fare, a difference that is not statistically significant. To express the finding in another way, where there are deviations from the available menu, the fan varies his selection of programs in much the same way as does the less enthusiastic viewer.

To test the proposition that what people say about television might be a clue to what they watch, we asked specific questions dealing with why they watch to begin with (Table 6-6) and the areas of programming they would like to have increased (Tables 6-7 and 6-8). These three tables again show remarkably little variation. The people who say they

table 6-5
Diet by Attitude toward TV (expressed in percentages of total minutes of TV watched by program type)

PROGRAM TYPE	RANK ON ATTITUDE SCALE	
	High	Medium & Low
Comedy-variety	26	25
Movies	20	19
Action	17	16
Sports	9	9
Light music	9	10
Light drama	2	2
News	13	16
Information and public affairs	3	2
Heavy drama	—	—
Religion	—	—
Heavy music	—	—
Base (Minutes): 100 percent = ...	67,290	245,790
N (Number of Viewers) = ...	61	283

135

table 6-6

"When you watch TV, how often does each of the following reasons apply?"

Diet by Response to "I Watch Because I Think I Can Learn Something" (expressed in percentages of total minutes of TV watched by program type)

	PERCENT WHO SAY			
PROGRAM TYPE	Never	Rarely	Occa-sionally	Usually
Comedy-variety	22	23	27	26
Movies	22	26	19	17
Action	19	17	16	16
Sports	10	10	9	8
Light music	11	8	10	9
Light drama	2	2	3	2
News	13	12	15	18
Information and public affairs	1	1	2	3
Heavy drama	—	—	—	—
Religion	—	—	—	1
Heavy music	—	—	—	—
Base (Minutes): 100 percent =	22,875	45,510	155,310	94,275
N (number of viewers)	(31)	(62)	(161)	(90)

usually watch television to learn something do watch news and information programming more than others, but only a little bit more. Those who feel there is not enough "food for thought" on television watch as many entertainment shows as the rest of the viewers. Those who want television stations (in Table 6-8) to concentrate on information programs spend only slightly more time watching such programs than those who want the "best entertainment," despite the fact that a great deal of informative fare is available in the Minneapolis–St. Paul area for those who could just switch the dial to another channel.

Obviously the differences that have been noted here among the various segments of the Minneapolis–St. Paul sample are not striking. What

table 6-7

Diet by the Desire Expressed for Programs That Provide "Food for Thought" (expressed in percentages of total minutes of TV watched by program type)

	PERCENT WHO SAY	
PROGRAM TYPE	Not Enough	Enough
Comedy-variety	26	26
Movies	20	17
Action	15	18
Sports	9	9
Light music	9	10
Light drama	2	2
News	16	16
Information and public affairs	2	2
Heavy drama	—	—
Religion	—	—
Heavy music	—	—
Base (Minutes): 100 percent = ...	187,710	98,625
N (number of viewers)	(200)	(106)

is interesting is the fact that they differ so little. Group characteristics and attitudes and expressed desires are not always predictive of behavior, as social scientists continue to find to their distress, but in most areas of human activity they are more predictive than they are here. The political scientist can make a fairly good guess about how a citizen will vote if he knows about his education and occupation, and a very good guess if he knows his political attitudes. But apparently to know such things and more about the television watcher gives us only a very slim reed upon which to base a prediction about what sort of a program he will watch. This may be, in part, because of the influence of others in the family on his choice of programs—a subject we treat in Chapter 7. But it may also be that views expressed about television are partly derived from a generalized and even stereotyped concept of the medium rather than from an examination and assessment of its actual content.

Since neither the characteristics of the viewers nor their expressed ideas about the medium seemed to make much difference in viewing we

137

table 6-8

"Generally speaking, would you say that television should provide more informational material or should it concentrate on providing the best entertainment possible?"

Diet by Preference for Information versus Entertainment Programs (expressed in percentages of total minutes of TV watched by program type)

	THOSE WHO SAY		
PROGRAM TYPE	More Information	Best Entertainment	Both
Comedy-variety	24	26	27
Movies	17	21	20
Action	16	17	15
Sports	11	8	8
Light music	8	10	9
Light drama	2	2	3
News	17	14	16
Information and public affairs	4	2	2
Heavy drama	—	—	—
Religion	—	—	—
Heavy music	—	—	—
Base (Minutes): 100 percent = .	83,055	151,350	82,875
N (number of viewers) = ...	(95)	(146)	(102)

tried one other type of variable—called here a "culture index," derived from a series of items about leisure-time activities. People who said they went to concerts, read books with some frequency, played a musical instrument, went out to meetings, lectures, or talks scored higher on the index than those who didn't. For our purposes here, we separated those with very high scores from the rest.

The 23 "high culture" people, it turned out, watched television somewhat less than those who scored lower; when they did watch, their viewing was distributed among program types in almost precisely the same way as the low-culture scorers, hardly a hair's breadth of difference between them except in the news and sports categories (Table 6-9).

table 6-9

Diet by Scores on a Culture Index (expressed in percentages of total minutes of TV watched by program type)

PROGRAM TYPE	THOSE RANKING ON CULTURE INDEX	
	Medium & Low	High
Comedy-variety	26	25
Movies	20	19
Action	16	17
Sports	9	5
Light music	10	10
Light drama	2	2
Information and public affairs	2	3
News	15	19
Heavy drama	—	—
Religion	—	1
Heavy music	—	—
Base (Minutes): 100 percent = ...	298,605	18,615
N (number of viewers)	(321)	(23)

THE MISSED OPPORTUNITIES

Our data permit one final comparison of people's characteristics and ideas versus their actual viewing. During two of the weeks in November there was one weekday hour of clear choice for viewers between information and entertainment programming. Between 9 and 10 on Tuesday evenings, one of the VHF stations carried the news-documentary program, *60 Minutes*. Also being shown, at the same time on the other three commercial stations, were *Marcus Welby* (a benign doctor and his motorcycle-riding colleague practicing medicine and human relations); *Run-for-Your-Life* (reruns of an action series); and a movie. The ARB ratings showed that *60 Minutes* was watched in about 11 percent of the households, *Marcus Welby* in about 22 percent, and a movie in about 19 percent. *Run-for-Your-Life* ran last with 3 percent, and the remainder of the households (45 percent of the sample) were not watching television during those particular hours.

table 6-10
Missed Opportunities by Education of Respondent

| | EDUCATION | | |
VIEWING	Less than College	College and Beyond	Total
Saw information program	10	11	11
Saw entertainment program (Welby) .	19	15	18
Saw something else*	19	13	17
Not watching	52	61	55
Base: 100 percent = ...	(167)	(62)	(229)

* *Run-for-Your-Life* and/or a movie.

This seems a fair enough competition; we are dealing only with the four commercial channels in order not to confound the findings by inclusion of the relatively ill-attended ETV channel, and we are pitting a well-regarded information program against a well-rated entertainment feature, in prime viewing time.

Tables 6-10 and 6-11 show the results for our subsample of 229 individuals on whom we had diary records for the two weeks. The propor-

table 6-11
Missed Opportunities by Preference for Information versus Entertainment

VIEWING	Want More Info.	Want Best Entertainment	Want Both	Total
Saw information program	13	8	13	11
Saw entertainment program (Welby)	19	14	23	18
Saw something else*	14	18	19	17
Not watching	54	60	45	55
Base: 100 percent = ...	(63)	(100)	(44)	(207)

* *Run-for-Your-Life* and/or a movie.

tion of viewers is not as high as the figures quoted above since we are dealing with individuals, and the ARB tallies are based on all members of the households who might be viewing.

The results here do not alter what we have learned before. Just about the same proportions of college and noncollege viewers saw the information program. Those who said that television should provide more information were slightly more apt to watch the information program, but they were also slightly more apt to watch *Marcus Welby*. The differences do not seem impressive.

This analysis of television viewing in one city adds confirmation to the conclusion of Chapter 3 that television's audience is a rather undifferentiated one. We note a few differences here and there between people's viewing—older people spend more time with news, men with sports, information seekers with information programs—but over-all the similarities seem much more pronounced than the variations. Some of the characteristics and attitudes of viewers may affect the amount of time they spend watching television—women in the Minneapolis–St. Paul sample for instance spend more time with TV than the men, even in the evening and weekend hours, but the distribution of programs they chose to watch remains about the same.

A few cautionary remarks should be made here. The findings are based on a small sample of viewers, in one city, selected from families who had been willing to cooperate in ARB's diary survey. Even though their answers to attitudinal questions are close to those we found in the national survey, we cannot say with confidence that they are representative of a nation of viewers. It is possible too that the categorization of programs into the eleven types may not have caught some qualitative differences among programs within each category. *Gunsmoke* may capture a different audience from *Run-for-Your-Life;* both were classified as "action" programs. *Red Skelton* and *Laugh-in* are both in the comedy-variety category, but they may draw different audiences. So it may be only among very broad areas of programming that such miniscule audience variations appear; another, more refined, set of categories of programs might have led to different results.

Nevertheless, there is a compelling consistency among the findings of the 1970 study, and between New York in 1960 and Minneapolis–St. Paul a decade later. The characteristics of viewers, their attitudes toward television, what they say they want on television—none of these factors seems to play a very important part in what people actually watch.

CHAPTER *7*

VIEWING IN THE FAMILY

This chapter will explore patterns of viewing within American families along a route leading from the location of the television set or sets in the house to the composition of family members who are likely to watch together. It will pursue the distribution of responsibility among them for choosing which programs to watch and discuss the opinions of parents about their children's viewing and the attempts they make to control it.

VIEWING PATTERNS

In its early days, the watching of television was often seen as an important new social activity; families would stay at home sharing the set as a focal point of conviviality, whereas without TV they would disperse to different individual activities. As far back as 1949, some sociologists noted that television was causing the development of subtle changes within the family as an institution. Riley, Cantwell, and Ruttiger pointed out in one article that long-term TV owners were feeling more family solidarity and a closing of the gap between adults and children as a result of television; but they also noted that it was not as mature as radio and that in the

143

case of the latter medium the early trends had not continued.[1] By the mid-fifties, perceptions of TV's role as a family medium did, in fact, become more ambivalent. Coffin posed the basic dilemma in *The American Psychologist* in 1955: "TV is both credited with increasing the family's fund of common experience and shared interests and blamed for decreasing its conversation and face-to-face interaction."[2] By 1969, Robinson had found that when people get used to having a television set, they are better able to watch it and do other things at the same time;[3] and in 1971, a report for the Surgeon General's Advisory Committee on Television and Social Behavior also concluded that there is interaction among family members during most of their joint viewing.[4]

To explore further the role of television in the family we started, early in our interview, by asking where the television sets were located in the house. And since to some extent at least, television viewing is a family activity, it should come as no great surprise that the sets are placed in rooms where family and friends get together (Table 7-1). In at least 90 percent of American households, it appears that the TV set or a set if there is more than one, is in the main sitting-around-in-the-evening room in the house, the living room or "family" room. A recent study by Lyle and Hoffman concurs: in their sample, the television set was located in the living room or family room in 87 percent of the cases.[5] The set is not likely to be in the bedroom among those families with only one set. But the chances are very good of finding one there when there are two or more sets in the family. In three- and four-set families, there is a television set in the living room, a set in one or two bedrooms, and in the recreation or playroom where the children tend to gather.

After discovering where the sets were placed in the house, we asked some additional questions in the national study to further investigate family viewing patterns. Was more than one person likely to watch each set? If so, who were they?

Rating services that collect statistics on actual viewing show that the better-known programs are generally watched by more than one person at each set. In our Minneapolis–St. Paul substudy, when we asked

---

[1] John Riley, Rank Cantwell, and Katherine Ruttiger, "Some Observations on the Social Effects of Television," *Public Opinion Quarterly*, Summer 1949 (Vol. 15 No. 2), p. 254.

[2] Thomas E. Coffin, "Television's Impact on Society," *The American Psychologist*, Vol. 10, No. 10, October 1955, pp. 630–41.

[3] John P. Robinson, "Television and Leisure Time," *Public Opinion Quarterly*, Summer 1969, pp. 210–222.

[4] Jack Lyle, "Television in Daily Life," *Television and Social Behavior*, op. cit.

[5] Jack Lyle and Heidi Hoffman, "Children's Use of Television and Other Media," in *Television and Social Behavior*, op cit.

table 7-1

"In what room is (this, each) set usually located in the house?"

Location of Sets in Single and Multiset Households

	The Only Set in One-Set Households	The Main Set in Multiset Households	The Additional Sets in Multi-set Households
Livingroom	76	63	7
Family room	16	22	11
Bedroom(s)	4	10	62
Recreation or play room ...	1	2	10
Kitchen	1	3	6
Dining room	1	1	2
Other room	—	—	2
No special location (portable)	—	—	1
Base (No. Sets): 100% = ..	(1036)	(738)	(952)
N (No. of households) = ..	(1036)	(738)	(738)

respondents "who else was watching television with you the last time you saw something on it," 71 percent said they viewed it with at least one other member of the household, and in our national sample, only 12 percent said that there "is no particular time when more than one person is likely to be watching TV."

The two most popular family groupings for viewing television are a husband and wife together and the entire family together. This general pattern can be seen in Table 7-2 which shows what happens in a one-set household.

Those cases that fall into the category of "no likely joint viewing" (14 percent) include some single-person households. To examine the extent of solitary viewing within more typical families, we can eliminate the single people and childless couples from our calculations and concentrate on those homes where we find a father, mother, and at least one child. Table 7-3 gives some idea of the extent to which multiple sets increase the likelihood of solitary viewing in the typical family.

In families with only one set, joint viewing is reported "likely" at some time of day, usually in the early evening, in 94 percent of the cases. In 6 percent of the cases, viewing by only one person is most likely. But

145

table 7-2

"Who usually watches the set (during the particular time when more than one person is likely to be watching it)?"

Likely Viewing Combinations in One-set Households

	Percent Who Say
No likely joint viewing	14
Husband-wife	33
Entire family	30
Children	7
Mother-children	7
Father-children	2
Other	7
Base (households): 100 percent =	(1036)

in the three- and four-set families, joint viewing is apt to take place in only two-thirds of the cases. It is probable that each of the sets in the multiset families is not used as much as the only set in a one-set family; so the finding of less-likely joint-viewing around particular sets does not necessarily mean that the *collective totality* of family viewing time in such households is necessarily reduced; it does mean that solitary viewing is increased. The second, third, and fourth sets are often located somewhere in the house where one person can get away from the others to watch by himself. In the three- and four-set family, there is apt to be a set that is designated "mine" by some family member.

table 7-3

Likelihood of Joint Viewing in One-set and Multiset Families

	Base: 100 percent =	Percent of Sets Around Which Joint Viewing Is:	
		Likely	Not Likely
One-set families	(1036)	94	6
Two-set families	(543)	80	20
Three-set families	(160)	66	34
Four-set families	(35)	65	35

The tendency for those extra sets to create opportunities for viewing television by oneself is hardly surprising. Perhaps that is why they were bought to begin with. Does the introduction of extra sets alter the frequency with which the husband and wife or the entire family are likely to watch television together? We can see what happens most clearly by separating the main set from the others. (The main set is the one which our respondents mentioned first, and in the multiset household it tends to be the one in the living room.)

table 7-4

"Likely" Joint Viewing in Single and Multiset Families (expressed in percentages of occasions for viewing)

Family Members Viewing Together:	In Single-set House-holds	IN MULTISET HOUSEHOLDS		
		Around the "Main" Set	All Sets Combined	Around the 2nd, 3rd, 4th, Sets Combined
Husband-wife	17	20	26	33
Entire family	55	49	34	12
Children	13	14	26	43
Mother-children ...	9	5	5	3
Father-children	4	10	7	4
Others	3	2	3	4
Base: 100 percent =	(443)	(367)	(613)	(246)

Extra sets in the household do make a difference in patterns of family viewing. The first two columns in Table 7-4 show that there are no marked changes in joint viewing in the single-set family or around the main set in the multiset family. In other words, the *main* set acts pretty much as the *only* set in the composition of the family members it brings together. However, in column three, which shows joint viewing around *all* sets combined in a multiset household, we find that viewing by the entire family declines and that there is more viewing together by children without their parents; and the fourth column shows that it is the children by themselves who are the major watchers of the second, third, or fourth set. These extra sets are now used for joint viewing by children 43 percent of

table 7-5
"Who usually watches the set (during the particular time mentioned when more than one person watches it)?"

Viewing Combinations (by race)

Percent Who Report Viewing by:	RACE	
	White	Black
Husband and Wife	50	43
Entire Family*	42	37
Mother and Child	8	20
Base: 100 percent = ...	(1151)	(91)

Viewing Combinations (by occupation of head of household)

Percent Who Report Viewing by:	OCCUPATION	
	White Collar	Blue Collar
Husband and Wife	48	33
Entire Family*	41	59
Mother and Child	10	7
Base: 100 percent = ...	(310)	(592)

* Defined as Married Couples with Children

the time and by the entire family only 12 percent of the time. Lyle and Hoffman's study also suggests that in multiset households, one set is "the children's set."[6]

   With extra television sets in the family, it would appear that more solitary watching takes place and that joint viewing tends to separate into smaller units, the children in one room and the parents in another. Is that extra set splitting up the family that may have been brought together because of the first one? It would be premature to take such a reading of the data, since there is still a great deal of joint family viewing around the *main* set, even in the multiset family. Furthermore, there is little justification for identifying the extra television set as a *cause* of alterations in family patterns. It is just as likely that causation, if any, flows in the opposite direction; the extra set may represent a desire for separated viewing and may be instrumental in fulfilling a pre-existent tendency in

6 Lyle and Hoffman, op. cit.

families toward separate pursuit of leisure-time activities. Questions of cause and effect aside, the phenomenon is worth watching. The time spent before the TV set is a major portion of the American's waking day and a major element in his interaction with other members of the family.

We have already seen that there are some variations in family viewing patterns influenced by the introduction of extra television sets. To a smaller degree, patterns are influenced by background characteristics of the families. Table 7-5 shows the three most frequent viewing combinations by race and occupation.

Husbands and wives tend to get together for their viewing in white-collar families, while blue-collar workers are more apt to corral the whole family before the set, and it is more common for mothers and children to watch together in black than in white families. But despite these variations, in most families there are three basic viewing patterns—*the entire family together, husband and wife viewing together* and *mothers watching with their children.*

WHO CONTROLS THE SET?

Concentrating on these three typical patterns of joint viewing, we asked the question: "Who usually decides what program to watch?" Table 7-6 shows a large amount of group or mutual decision-making reported in each

table 7-6

Who Usually Decides What Programs to Watch on the Set?
(during particular time mentioned when more than one person watches it)

	VIEWERS		
PERCENT WHO REPORT DECISIONS MADE BY:	Mother and Children	Husband and Wife	Entire Family*
Group or mutual decision	27	53	42
Husband/father	—	28	27
Wife/mother	37	18	10
Child/children	33	—	17
Other, NA	3	1	4
Base: 100 percent = ...	(100)	(508)	(347)

* Defined as married couples with children.

of the three major viewing arrangements. A number of respondents replied "no one in particular" to this question. We classified this answer as a group decision, although in some cases it may have indicated habitual viewing where no one had to decide about an individual program—the same thing was watched every Wednesday night.

When mothers and children view together, the mother is reported as the decision-maker in only 37 percent of the cases. The children decide by themselves 33 percent of the time; the mother and children together, 27 percent. Husbands tend to make the decisions rather than their wives when the two are watching together; and fathers tend to decide for the family more than mothers. The children's role is substantial in both of the situations that involve them. They make the decisions almost as frequently as their mothers, and even when the whole family is together they are reported as sole decision-makers in 17 percent of the cases and are presumably joining in the mutual decisions in another 42 percent of the cases.

These are the modal patterns in a generalized American family; some distinct differences appear if we divide the sample by such sociologically relevant characteristics as education, income, occupation, or race. In Tables 7-7 and 7-8 we can compare families of two *occupational*

table 7-7
Who Decides What Program to Watch on the Set (by occupation of head of household)

	VIEWERS					
	Mother and Children		Husband and Wife		Entire Family*	
PERCENT WHO REPORT DECISION MADE BY:	White Collar	Blue Collar	White Collar	Blue Collar	White Collar	Blue Collar
Group or mutual decision	26	20	66	43	39	43
Husband/father ...	—	—	22	36	31	26
Wife/mother	47	34	11	20	11	11
Child/children	21	43	—	—	17	17
Other, NA	5	2	1	2	2	4
Base: 100 percent = .	(38)	(44)	(177)	(195)	(121)	(196)

* Defined as married couples with children.

table 7-8
Who Decides What to Watch on the Set (by race)

	VIEWERS			
	Husband and Wife		Entire Family*	
DECISIONS MADE BY:	White	Black	White	Black
Group or mutual decision	53	58	44	32
Husband/father	29	18	28	19
Wife/mother	17	23	11	7
Child/children	—	—	16	32
Other, NA	1	3	3	10
Base: 100 percent = ...	(462)	(40)	(309)	(31)

* Defined as married couples with children.

categories—white-collar and blue-collar workers—and of two *races*—white and black.

In one respect, the role of the children is particularly pronounced in the families of blue-collar workers. When they are watching television together with their mothers, the children are likely to decide which programs to watch in twice as many cases as in white-collar families (43 percent compared to 21 percent). When the whole family is viewing together, the children in blue-collar families either make or participate in decisions to a slightly greater extent, in 60 percent of the cases as compared to 56 percent for the children in white-collar families. There are more mutual decisions between the white-collar husbands and wives (66 percent compared to 43 percent for the blue-collar families) and a slightly greater decision-making role for white-collar fathers in family viewing (31 percent compared to 26 percent).

There are also differences in family viewing patterns between whites and blacks. Table 7-8 deals only with husband, wife, and entire family viewing since there were not enough cases of black mother-child viewing (because of the small sample of blacks) to justify tabulations. Even the figures which are presented are statistically unreliable and should be interpreted only as possible indicators of race differences in TV decision-making. Black women are the decision-makers more often than their husbands when the two are watching together—23 percent compared to

151

18 percent. Among white families, the husband makes the decisions more often than the wife—29 percent compared to 17 percent. The greatest difference again occurs in the child's role as decision-maker. In black families they decide about programs to watch in 32 percent of the cases when families are watching together. In white families they decide in 16 percent of the cases. In fact, black children are reported as making more of the decisions than their mothers and fathers combined in this very small sample of black families.

The children's role would appear to be a function of the family's general socioeconomic status—they play a larger part in black than in white families, and in the blue-collar than in white-collar families. Other data not shown here indicate their more dominant role in less-educated and in poor families, as one would expect from the interrelation of these variables. These are points worth keeping in mind as we proceed to examine other aspects of family viewing.

THE PERCEIVED EFFECTS ON CHILDREN

There are probably more experts espousing theories on the effects of television on children than on any other subject related to the medium. In addition to the cocktail-party expertise, there is a growing body of knowledge on television's effects on children, based upon empirical studies.[7] The present work cannot add much to the public debate nor directly buttress the research: we are not dealing with effects but with people's *beliefs* about effects and, to some small extent, with the question of how these beliefs influence the control that parents exercise over their children's viewing.

Our discussion of perceived effects follows the Steiner questionnaire, permitting some 1960–1970 comparisons, and then branches off into new areas of inquiry which were suggested by the 1960 findings. Like Steiner, we started with a general question which separates the "pros" and the "cons" on the issue of television as a beneficial or harmful force (Chart 7-1).

There would appear to be a modest trend toward *greater* approval of television for children in the population at large, a higher proportion in 1970 saying that children are "better off" with it. But this is a trend

---

[7] Eli A. Rubenstein, George A. Comstock, and John P. Murray, eds., *Television and Social Behavior*. A Technical Report to the Surgeon General's Scientific Advisory Committee on Television and Social Behavior. Vols. 1–5. Washington, D.C.: U.S. Government Printing Office, Department of Health, Education and Welfare, 1972.

chart 7-1

Percent Who Say Better Off:

"There has been a lot of discussion about the possible effects of television on children. Taking everything into consideration, would you say that children are better off with television or better off without television?"

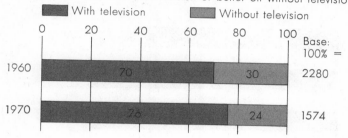

that does not apply equally to all groups in the population. The proportion of "pros" among those with only a grade school education remains steady, while the proportion among the college educated increases from 61 to 78 percent as shown in Chart 7-2.

Steiner was no doubt puzzled by the lack of a stronger relationship between education and beliefs about over-all effects on children. In question after question about television in the 1960 survey, the better educated indicated a much lower opinion of the medium than the less educated. Why then, when it comes to effects on children, were the college graduate and the fellow who quit after grade school so much more in general agreement? Steiner dealt with the problem in two ways. First, he showed that another characteristic, parenthood, was more important than education in separating the "pros" from the "cons." Second, he suggested that the better and the less-well educated, though close in their general assessment, were not really in full agreement about what being "better off" means. We will follow these two lines of reasoning with the 1970 data, which are even more puzzling, since now we see a slight inversion of the usual relationship between education and attitudes toward television.

Table 7-9 provides further elaboration of the observed trend of more college-educated adults liking TV for their children, by separating the parents of children under fifteen—the group for whom the question is most salient—from all others in the sample.

If we first look at the 1960 differences between parents and others in the first and third columns, we see, as Steiner noted, that parents think more highly of television for children than do nonparents at all educational levels. Then, observing the differences between 1960 and 1970, we can see some of the components of the over-all trend toward greater approval

153

chart 7-2

Perceptions of Children as Better Off with and without Television by Education of Respondent

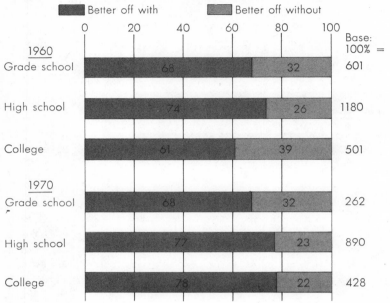

■ Better off with   ▨ Better off without

		Base: 100% =
1960		
Grade school	68 / 32	601
High school	74 / 26	1180
College	61 / 39	501
1970		
Grade school	68 / 32	262
High school	77 / 23	890
College	78 / 22	428

of television for children. Among all but one group there is an increase in the proportion saying "better off with." The one deviant group is the grade school parents who move in the opposite direction—away from "better off with"—with a higher proportion of them saying "better off without" television in 1970 than in 1960. It is the college-educated parent who in 1970 gives television the highest endorsement of all, 81 percent saying "better off with," and the college-educated, both parents and non-parents are the ones who have most substantially improved their ratings of television for children. The grade school educated, who are most apt to be superfans of television in general, give it the lowest rating of all.

We will return to these reverse shifts in a moment, after examining some further questions that Steiner asked in his interviews and which we repeated in the second study. The "pros" ("better off with") were asked to describe some of the main advantages they saw in television for children, followed by a similar question on disadvantages. The "cons" ("better off without") were asked the two questions in reverse order. Tables 7-10 and 7-11 allow comparisons between parents and nonparents and between education groups for the two years.

table 7-9

Perceptions That Children Are Better Off with Television (by education and parental status)

PERCENT WHO SAY CHILDREN ARE BETTER OFF WITH TELEVISION

	Parents of Children Under 15				Others				Total			
	1960		1970		1960		1970		1960		1970	
	%	N	%	N	%	N	%	N	%	N	%	N
Grade school	75	207	68	67	65	394	68	196	68	601	68	262
High school	77	649	79	446	70	531	72	444	74	1180	77	890
College	68	262	81	229	54	239	75	199	61	501	78	428
Total percent	75		79		65		72		70		76	
Base: 100 percent =	(1118)		(742)		(1164)		(839)		(2282)		(1580)	

155

table 7-10
"What do you think are some of the main advantages of television for children?"

The Advantages of TV for Children by Respondent's General Attitude (Pro or Con) toward Television for Children*

PERCENT WHO MENTION:	1960 PARENTS		1960 OTHERS		1960 Total	1970 Total	1970 PARENTS		1970 OTHERS	
	Pros	Cons	Pros	Cons			Pros	Cons	Pros	Cons
Education	74	49	72	45	65	80	85	69	85	62
Baby-sitting	34	21	31	13	28	16	17	13	18	9
Entertainment	21	15	23	8	19	22	27	20	21	17
Programs good generally ..	4	17	6	16	8	2	2	2	2	2
Stimulates socializing	2	—	1	—	1	2	3	—	2	2
Adult supervision necessary .	4	2	10	4	6	2	2	—	2	1
Other, general	1	4	1	4	2	4	3	6	2	6
Base: 100% = ...	(858)	(292)	(781)	(419)	(2350)	(1592)	(589)	(159)	(607)	(237)

* Multiple response item: percentages do not necessarily add up to 100 percent.

The advantages.—The gross ten-year changes in the types of advantages that adults see in television for children can be found by comparing the two "total" columns. The *increase* in mentions of educational benefits, and the *decrease* in number of people who see television as a convenient baby-sitter for children, are both marked. Fewer people now than before refer to programs themselves when they discuss advantages (when they do, *Sesame Street* and *Walt Disney* lead the way), and in 1970 fewer parents saw a need for adult supervision while children are watching.

table 7-11
Advantages of Television for Children* (by education of respondent)

PERCENT WHO MENTION:	1960				1970			
	Grade School	High School	Col-lege	Total 1960	1970 Total	Grade School	High School	Col-lege
Education	58	66	72	65	80	69	80	86
Baby-sitting	32	31	18	28	16	19	18	9
Entertainment	15	21	18	19	23	18	26	21
Programs good	8	8	8	8	2	2	2	1
Stimulates socializing	2	1	2	1	2	2	2	2
Adult supervision necessary	5	5	7	6	2	1	1	2
Other	2	2	3	2	4	3	3	6
Base: 100 percent = .	(601)	(1180)	(501)	(2282)	(1588)	(266)	(894)	(429)

* Multiple response item: percentages do not necessarily add up to 100 percent.

The greatest advantage of television for children, according to the adults, is its educational benefit. Television, it is felt, provides moral lessons, and teaches children to sort out right from wrong:

"They have a chance to look at the good and bad and decide what's best for themselves."

"When they see crime and the one that does the crime gets caught, that helps children to stay out of bad company."

157

Or it broadens the child's horizons:

> "I think television makes children see how other people live. I think
> they get exposed to many new, different ways of life, they certainly
> can learn about politics and world affairs."

> "They're put right out into the world rather than with just their
> own neighbors, quicker. It used to be the Joneses that were your
> neighbors. Now the world is."

Or it teaches specific skills:

> "It increases their vocabulary and their general knowledge, defi-
> nitely."

> "They learn to express themselves at an early age."

Or it teaches a lot about everything:

> "Children are becoming more informed about everything. They see
> sports, different countries, children's movies and *Sesame Street*.
> Also they become informed on bad things and sometimes being
> informed can be good for them. Specials on drug addiction are
> helpful. If they are drug addicts they might be impressed and learn
> from the mistakes of others."

In 1960, Steiner found the "baby-sitting" functions of television as
the second greatest advantage of TV for children. Typical responses such
as "it keeps them occupied, they stay out of trouble" and "it keeps them
out of my hair" were apt to be accompanied by mentions of educational
benefits, especially by the college-educated parents. As Steiner notes,
there is "some defensiveness among the well-educated TV-dependent
parent" who may mention educational benefits in order to justify the less-
acceptable baby-sitting response. By 1970, this phenomenon persists only
in very rare cases within the depleted ranks of those who mention baby-
sitting advantages. A college graduate with two children says, for instance:

> "They learn a lot from TV. It keeps them occupied while I get my
> work done."

A far more frequent response in 1970 combines a mention of the
entertaining nature of television for children with its educational benefits:

"TV is entertaining for children, like the Walt Disney shows; and through TV they learn that adults are not all as they appear to be, making the kids less gullible. I approve of television by far over movies and the theatre."

"I think television is educational for children. I think it gives them views on all parts of the world and I also think it is entertaining; children need to stay busy."

"It is cheap entertainment, and it provides educational information at the same time."

The educational advantage, either accompanied by another benefit or by itself, pervades the answers to this question in 1970. Parents perceive of television for children as *primarily* an educator, with some entertainment and a small amount of baby-sitting thrown in. Comparing the 1960 and 1970 data, one gets the impression that the American parent has fired the *baby-sitter,* and hired instead a *nanny* whose major assignment is to teach the children everything from ABC's to moral principles.

The disadvantages.—Americans, whether experienced in parenthood or not, find no difficulty in talking about television's effects on children—including the negative effects; even those who saw television as generally beneficial had something to say about its disadvantages. In 1960 and again in 1970 a large number of themes emerged from their answers, as we can see in Table 7-12.

Just about as many people in 1970 as in 1960 feel that children may "see things they shouldn't" by watching television; but some of those things that they shouldn't see have apparently changed in ten years' time. There is just the same amount of violence noted on TV in 1970 as there was a decade earlier (the summary figure for "violence" includes programs with crime, gangsters, and horror as well as the dire, dangerous, and bloody). But immorality—sex, seminudity, smoking and drinking, bad language—is seen increasingly as harmful to children. Here are some comments from the interviews:

"Some of the language used, the cursing for example, isn't good for the ears of small children."

"There are programs that show women nearly naked. I don't approve of young children being exposed to nudity."

"Too much sex. Half-nude girls and their movements. Men's movements also, especially when singing."

table 7-12

"What do you think are some of the main disadvantages of television for children?"

Disadvantages of Television for Children* by Parental Status and General Attitude (Pro and Con) toward Television for Children

	1960					1970				
	PARENTS		OTHERS				PARENTS		OTHERS	
PERCENT WHO MENTION:	Pros	Cons	Pros	Cons	1960 Total	1970 Total	Pros	Cons	Pros	Cons
See things they shouldn't:	46	55	48	64	51	52	48	55	50	64
Violence, horror ...	26	32	28	40	30	30	27	32	30	35
Crime, gangsters ..	7	8	11	13	10	8	6	10	9	12
Sex, suggestiveness, vulgarity ...	4	7	4		5	11	10	12	11	13
Smoking, drinking, dope	2	2		3	2	5	4	5	6	7
Adult themes	2	3		3	2	9	6	11	10	12
Harmful or sinful products advertised	1			1	—	1	1	1	—	1	1
Wrong values or moral codes			2	5	3	8	8	11	8	9
Other, general		1	8	9	8	2	3	5	2	5
Keeps them from doing things they should ..	34	51	31	41	36	30	29	40	26	34
Programs bad, general.	10	9	8	13	10	2	2	6	2	3
Other, program content	3	9	2	6	4	6	7	10	5	6
Physical harm	3	7	4	8	5	5	3	4	5	7
Advertising too effective	2	3	1	—	1	2	3	3	2	3
Other	2	3	1	3	2	5	6	5	5	3
Base: 100 percent =	(858)	(292)	(781)	(419)	(2350)	(1583)	(586)	(157)	(604)	(236)

* Multiple response item: percentages do not necessarily add up to 100 percent.

"It emphasizes too much of the racial· situations and sex; these topics are much too old for young children. TV is becoming too much like the movies. There's just a lot that is not suitable for children."

The increase in the accusation of immorality may be a clue to the problem of the turned-off, less-educated adults—those with only a grade school education—some of whom are starting to see television as bad for children while other groups are finding its influence more beneficial than they did before. Table 7-13 below gives us an opportunity to examine (in

table 7-13
Disadvantages of Television for Children (by education of respondent)

PERCENT WHO MENTION:	1960				1970			
	Grade School	High School	Col- lege	1960 Total	1970 Total	Grade School	High School	Col- lege
See things they shouldn't (any of below):	56	54	53	54	53	56	53	52
Violence								
Violence, horror ..	32	28	31	30	31	32	30	32
Crime, gangsters .	11	10	8	10	9	13	9	5
Morality								
Sex, suggestiveness, bad language ..	5	5	4	5	12	12	13	9
Smoking, drinking, dope	2	1	2	2	9	10	9	8
Adult themes, know too much too soon	1	2	3	2	9	9	9	8
Harmful products advertised	—	1	1	1	—	—	—	—
Wrong values of moral codes taught	1	3	7	3	8	7	8	9
Other	5	7	6	6	3	4	3	4
Base: 100 percent = .	(601)	(1180)	(501)	(2282)	(1544)	(243)	(879)	(422)

both 1960 and 1970) the accusation of immorality, along with other "disadvantages" by the education level of the critics.

It turns out that in 1970 the accusations of immoral content are fairly evenly spread among the educational groups, coming just a bit more from the lower educated than from the higher. It is hardly enough of a finding to explain the shift by the lower-educated members of the sample against the popular current, since the mentions of immorality are still small in number; however, it may be a factor. The television depiction of

table 7-14

"Can you think of any actual example where some child you know or have heard about has benefited from television (asked of those who are *pro* TV for children)?"

"Can you think of an actual example where some child you know or have heard of has been harmed or has done something harmful as a result of television (asked of those who are *con* TV for children)?"

Examples of Benefit, Harm Given (by parental status of respondent)

	1960			1970		
PERCENT WHO:	Mothers	Fathers	1960 Total	1970 Total	Mothers	Fathers
Give example of benefit (among those who say children are better off *with* TV)	35	34	34	43	49	36
Base: 100 percent = ..	(460)	(398)	(858)	(562)	(293)	(269)
Give example of harm (among those who say children are better off *without* TV)	29	19	24	12	16	8
Base: 100 percent = ..	(164)	(128)	(292)	(153)	(82)	(71)

crime also appears to be somewhat more on the minds of the less educated in 1970—otherwise the differences among educational groups are hardly noticeable.

In addition to expressing feelings about television's virtues and vices for children, the respondents in both surveys were asked to cite concrete examples: for "pros," examples of a real benefit; for the "cons," examples of actual harm. Evidence of benefits increased while proof of harm decreased, as Table 7-14 shows, thus confirming a ten-year trend toward increased approval of television for children. In 1960, among parents who said that children were better off *with* television, 34 percent could cite examples of benefits; in 1970, 43 percent gave examples. Among the "cons" who thought that children were better off *without* television, the proportion who gave examples of harmful effects decreased from 24 to 12 percent.

The examples of benefits in 1970 were almost entirely educational —a little girl who learned the pledge of allegiance by watching *Romper Room;* a nine-year-old who picked up Spanish words through Spanish programs on an educational network; and many cases of numbers and letters taught to younger children by *Sesame Street.* "*Walt Disney,*" says one mother, "was responsible for my son having a vocabulary of 100 words at one year."

The examples of harm were "educational" in a different sense and were frequently attributed to the news programs on television rather than to the entertainment features. One nonparent cited a "kid out there in Arizona who heard about this guy in Texas killing all those people. He wanted to get his name in the paper and tried the same thing." Violence, often known through hearsay, predominated among the examples of harm; the complaint of immorality, curiously, is less frequently cited, but it does emerge occasionally:

> "No, I can't think of any. Oh yes, my nephew Mark is three years old and says to his mother 'let me kiss you like they kiss on TV.' "

GOOD AND BAD PROGRAMS FOR CHILDREN

The efforts that have been made over the past ten years to develop new programs for children, especially in the public broadcasting sector, is reflected in the parents' reply to a question concerning the best programs for their own children. In 1970, as compared to 1960, the choices have generally shifted to categories of programs explicitly designed for children as shown in Table 7-15.

Programs categorized as "children's variety, dramatic, adventure," which include, for example, *Walt Disney,* slightly increased in their proportion of the mentions. But programs in the "school, kindergarten" area, (for example, *Sesame Street*) soared in parental popularity; they were mentioned by 40 percent of the parents in 1970 as compared with 15 percent ten years earlier. Westerns, not too popular as fare for the young in 1960, declined further in popularity in 1970, as indeed they dropped in appearances on the screen.

The distribution of choices in both years and especially in 1970

table 7-15

"Which of the programs your (child watches/children watch) do you think are the best programs for (him, her, them)?"

PERCENT OF PARENTS WHO MENTION:*	1960	1970
Children's variety, dramatic, adventure	39	48
Cartoons	32	28
School, kindergarten	14	40
Adult shows, entertainment	15	19
Westerns	10	3
Sports	4	5
Teen-age dance	4	1
Other	6	4
Base: 100 percent = ...	(1170)	(813)

MOST FREQUENTLY MENTIONED PROGRAMS BY PARENTS

1960	N	%	1970	N	%
Captain Kangaroo	217	19	Sesame Street	220	30
Lassie	178	15	Walt Disney	167	23
Walt Disney	144	12	Lassie...............	80	11
Romper Room	115	10	Captain Kangaroo	68	9
Father Knows Best	115	10	Wild Kingdom	53	7
Huckleberry Hound ...	78	7	Jacques Cousteau	53	7
Popeye..............	71	6	Romper Room........	42	6
Dennis the Menace	65	6	National Geographic Specials...........	30	4

* Multiple response item: percentages do not necessarily add up to 100 percent.

suggests that the best-regarded programs are those that are designed to educate and not just to entertain. *Sesame Street* leads the list of favorite programs in 1970 despite the fact that half the sample of parents could not receive an educational television station. Other new programs on the most favored list—*Wild Kingdom, Jacques Cousteau,* and *National Geographic Specials*—all have strong educational components. This is quite consistent with the finding reported above that education is seen as the most important advantage of television for children.

The condemned programs, on the other hand—those that parents "aren't too happy about"—tend to be adult fare. In 1960, Westerns were most frequently mentioned. In 1970, the largest number of bad programs mentioned were also those with "adult" themes—too old for the children. *Dark Shadows*, now off the air was too intense emotionally, too scary; *Laugh-in* is too explicit, shows too much skin; it is too sophisticated (Table 7-16).

The violence theme recurs in 1970, as can be seen in the "violent adult shows" and "violent children's shows" categories and in the relatively frequent mentions of *The Three Stooges* and *Mod Squad*. It is no more pronounced than in 1960, when many objected to westerns which usually portray gun-slinging and violence. The major new concern is that *adult* programming is not proper TV material for the eyes of the young viewer.

table 7-16
"Which of the programs your (child watches/children watch) aren't you too happy about?"

PERCENT OF PARENTS WHO MENTION:*	1960	1970
Westerns	20	4
Violence, horror, general	19	13
Violent children's shows	9	11
Children's shows, other	10	13
Violent adult shows	9	11
Adult shows, shows with adult themes	5	20
Other	6	6
Base: 100 percent =	(1170)	(813)

PROGRAMS MOST FREQUENTLY MENTIONED BY PARENTS

1960	N	%	1970	N	%
Three Stooges	103	9	Dark Shadows	51	7
Untouchables	37	3	Laugh-In	40	6
77 Sunset Strip	20	2	Three Stooges	30	4
Popeye	19	2	Mod Squad	27	4

* Multiple response item: percentages do not necessarily add up to 100 percent.

SPECIFIC EFFECTS

In answer to questions about advantages and disadvantages of television for children, people did not necessarily talk directly about *effects* on children. They may have mentioned programs as being "good" or "bad," or may have seen an advantage in keeping a child occupied while the housework was getting done, or thought the child was exposed to some bad language. Effects can be inferred in such cases, but they are not explicit.

To more directly address the issue of effect—or more precisely a few specific hypothesized effects—we asked a series of questions about children who watch television a lot and those who watch very little—what sort of effect do adults think television watching has? The questions were phrased to elicit responses on two dimensions. First, does it make any difference at all how much a child views (for example, in his getting ahead in school)? Second, if an effect is perceived, does it favor the child who watched a lot or the one who watches less often? A third element appears in answers to these questions: some respondents say that "it depends" on the characteristics of the children (young or old, girl or boy, bright or dull) or on what and when the children watch. (Table 7-17)

In capsule form, here are the findings of what people think television helps children do:

"*To be better informed*"—Not only is television thought to be relevant here but the direction of its effects is clear. It favors the child who watches television a lot, according to 63 percent of all the adults as compared to 6 percent who say that children who watch little are better informed about the outside world.

"*To read more books*"—Television is thought to be highly relevant —mainly as an impediment—to such literary pursuits by children. Those who watch it very little are thought to have the distinct advantage over the heavy viewers.

"*To do better in school*"—Television is thought to be relevant to the question by most of the sample, with the light viewers slightly favored. To a fair degree (19 percent of the sample) whether television watching is a scholastic advantage or deficit is thought to depend on the characteristics of the child or on the rules applied to his viewing by parents—"as long as they get to bed on time."

"*To become better all around persons*"—This question was included as a summary item—total effects on the total person. Most people think that television viewing doesn't make much difference in producing such over-all effects.

"*To grow up in better health*"—This also doesn't appear as a relevant issue to most people in assessing TV's effects on children. Among those who think it is relevant, the light viewer—whose eyes are not strained by staring at the screen or who gets outside to play in the fresh air—is thought to be better off.

"*Getting into trouble*"—Television appears to be *least* relevant as

table 7-17

"Now, a few questions on the specific effects television might have in making some children act or behave differently from others: Who, do you think, are likely to do better in school, get in trouble, read more books, etc., children who watch a lot of television or children who watch very little; or do you think the amount of watching TV doesn't make much difference in how they do in school, how much trouble they get into, etc.?"

WHICH CHILDREN ARE MORE LIKELY:*		Percent
To be better informed about what is going on in the world?	"Not much difference"	20
	"It depends"	11
	"Those who watch TV a lot"	63
	"Those who watch TV very little"	6
To read more books?	"Not much difference"	29
	"It depends"	6
	"Those who watch TV a lot"	10
	"Those who watch TV very little"	55
To do better in school?	"Not much difference"	30
	"It depends"	19
	"Those who watch TV a lot"	21
	"Those who watch TV very little"	30
To grow up as better all-around persons?	"Not much difference"	53
	"It depends"	11
	"Those who watch TV a lot"	19
	"Those who watch TV very little"	17
To grow up in better health?	"Not much difference"	53
	"It depends"	9
	"Those who watch TV a lot"	7
	"Those who watch TV very little"	32
To get into trouble?	"Not much difference"	58
	"It depends"	15
	"Those who watch TV a lot"	19
	"Those who watch TV very little"	9

Base: 100 percent varies from item to item (1832–1843) depending on NA's.

*The questions have been reordered from highest to lowest relevance of TV (based on the proportion who answered "TV doesn't make much difference").

a factor contributing to children's propensity for getting into trouble. Only 28 percent of the adult sample believes that television viewing makes much of a difference one way or the other. For 19 percent, the heavier-viewing child is in greater jeopardy, presumably because of bad characters on the screen who might be emulated. In the view of about half that number (9 percent), the heavy-viewing child has the *advantage;* television presumably keeps him off the street where trouble occurs.

There are some slight variations to these composite pictures of television's effects. Parents, for example, see television as being somewhat *less* relevant as an influence on children in relation to all of the items, whether they are phrased as potential benefits ("do better in school") or as possible detriments ("getting into trouble"). The proportion of parents saying that television "doesn't make much difference" is slightly but consistently higher. We probably should not assume from this that parents have less concern than others about television's role in the rearing of the young. It may simply be that experience has revealed to them other forces that are more important in shaping their children's behavior.

The amount of schooling the respondents have had appears to make

table 7-18

TV's Perceived Effects on Children (by education of parent)

	Parent's Education		
	Grade School	High School	College
a. WHICH DO BETTER IN SCHOOL:			
Percent who say:			
TV doesn't make much difference	39	31	26
It depends	12	17	25
Those who watch a lot	22	21	22
Those who watch very little	27	31	27
b. WHICH ARE MORE APT TO GET INTO TROUBLE:			
Percent who say:			
TV doesn't make much difference	47	61	57
It depends	12	14	17
Those who watch a lot	30	17	17
Those who watch very little	11	8	7
Base: 100 percent =	(84)	(478)	(240)

little difference in the assessment of TV's effects on most questions. The less educated and better educated, however, do differ in their responses to two key items—television's effect on the child's performance in school and on the likelihood of his "getting into trouble"—as Table 7-18 shows.

Television as an influence on the children's formal education appears as a *more relevant* factor to the college-educated parents than to those with less education, who tend to feel that it "doesn't make much difference." At the same time, more of the college-educated parents answer that "it depends." One parent says: "It depends on the age of the child; in the early years it helps." Several say that television is helpful "as long as they don't stay up too late." Many say it depends on the programs the children are allowed to see. These parents recognize the potential dangers of television but seem to know what can be done to mitigate them.

Television as an influence on children's propensity for trouble, on the other hand, is a matter of concern to proportionally more of the grade school parents than of those with higher education. Fewer of the grade school educated say that television doesn't make much difference here, whereas on all the other items they tend to minimize television's influence. But there is little evidence in their replies that they consider it a factor over which they could exercise parental influence. One gets the impression that the college-educated parents have matters a bit better under control—or think they do—in an area where television seems to them to be especially influential. Where the grade school parents are more worried than others ("getting into trouble"), the potential for control is not as evident from the answers. Very few of them say, for instance, that it depends on the sort of programs children watch.

We may now return to an earlier theme—the reverse trends that appeared when we separated our sample into educational groups—the college-educated parent becoming more enthusiastic about television for the children and the grade school parent becoming less sanguine. It seems that the educated and less-educated parent see most of the same advantages and disadvantages in television, but in different proportions and with a different force. The college-educated parent sees education as the particularly salient factor in his assessment of television's effects, and gives less importance to the trouble-making propensities of the medium. The increase over ten years in the proportion of college educated who noticed educational advantages along with their felt ability, exercised or not, to control any deleterious educational effects could partially explain their increased feeling that children are generally "better off with" television.

The less educated, on the other hand, worry more about their children getting into trouble; they also observe a bit more inducement to trouble via television—programs which they tend to see as depicting crime, violence, moral turpitude—when they talk about disadvantages for children. One might expect them to have a lower assessment of television's over-all advantages for children.

PARENTAL CONTROL

It could be that if parents are increasingly seeing television as bene-ficial to children, they might be ready to relax even more the regulations they apply to their children's viewing. This does not appear to be the case. The parents of 1970 tell us that they are a bit stricter than their counterparts a decade earlier. A slightly higher proportion say they have "definite rules" and more of them report that their "kids decide with minor exceptions" (Table 7-19).

table 7-19
"Even though they're not always enforced 100 percent, are there any rules or regulations in your house about when and what your (child, children) watch, or do you let (him, her, them) make their own decisions?"

PERCENT WHO SAY:	1960	1970
We have definite rules	41	43
We try, we make an effort	6	5
Children decide with minor exceptions	4	14
We have no rules; children decide	30	31
Don't need rules—children too young	7	6
No answer, all other—rules not mentioned in response, etc.	12	2
Base: 100 percent (Parents) . . . . (1170)		(813)

These are, however, small changes and are probably merely a re-flection of the fact that parents are on the whole better educated than they were ten years ago, and better-educated parents (then and now) are more apt to have rules for their children—or at least they say they do. Forty-six percent of the 1970 college-educated parents say they have definite rules about their children's viewing as compared to 25 percent of the grade school parents. Similar variations by education appear in the 1960 figures. In 1960 and 1970, a substantial proportion of families re-ported leaving their children under 15 to their own devices. In both years, there were marked differences between educational groups. In 1970, 53 percent of the children with grade school parents were allowed to go it on their own, while only 27 percent of children with college-educated parents did not have TV-related rules (Table 7-20).

table 7-20

"Even though they're not always enforced 100 percent, are there any rules or regulations in your home about when and what your children watch or do you let (him, her, them) make their own decisions?"

BY EDUCATION OF PARENT

PERCENT WHO SAY:	1960				1970			
	Grade School	High School	College	1960 Total	Total 1970	Grade School	High School	College
We have definite rules	34	40	47	40	43	25	43	46
We try, we make an effort	3	5	8	5	5	6	4	6
Children decide with minor exceptions . .	2	5	4	4	14	10	15	13
We have no rules; children decide . . .	51	28	20	30	31	53	30	27
Don't need rules; children too young . . .	3	9	8	7	6	1	7	6
No answer, all other, rules not mentioned in response, etc. . .	7	14	13	12	2	6	2	2
Base: 100 percent = .	(230)	(703)	(275)	(1208)	(808)	(84)	(481)	(243)

SPECIFIC RULES

In the 1970 survey, we asked parents to talk about one specific child in the family, whose age varied from interview to interview between four and twelve years. We then asked about several TV-watching rules, selected from those that seemed to appear frequently, according to comments made by Steiner's respondents ten years before. The results for parents with children in various age groups are shown in Table 7-21.

table 7-21

"Here are some things parents have told us they do with their children about TV. Taking just one of your children, do you or your (husband, wife) often, occasionally, or never:"

	AGE OF CHILD:		
	4–6 yrs. (N = 197)	7–9 yrs. (N = 217)	10–12 yrs. (N = 189)
Rules about Viewing Time			
Restrict Amount of Viewing			
Often	30	39	34
Occasionally	27	25	27
Never	43	36	39
Set Special Hours			
Often	41	48	46
Occasionally	26	18	22
Never	32	34	32
Rules about Program Content			
Decide What Programs They Can Watch			
Often	45	37	46
Occasionally	28	35	38
Never	27	27	11
Change Channel When Program Is Objectionable			
Often	40	27	30
Occasionally	30	36	40
Never	31	29	31
Forbid Watching of Certain Programs			
Often	39	39	52
Occasionally	27	29	22
Never	35	32	25
Encouragement of Viewing			
Encourage Child to Watch to Keep Him Occupied			
Often	18	13	7
Occasionally	32	29	23
Never	50	58	71
Encourage Child to Watch to Keep Him at Home			
Often	9	10	5
Occasionally	9	14	15
Never	82	76	80

From what their parents say, it appears that many children, but by no means all of them, have to contend with restrictions and controls during all the years from four to twelve. At any time during those nine years, the hours they can watch may be limited, programs may be picked by a parent, and other programs forbidden—even switched off if they are thought to be objectionable. The older child, almost a teen-ager, is generally more apt to be restricted in his television viewing than the younger, and his programs are more apt to be selected by his parents. The four-or five-year-old may actually be encouraged to watch when he would rather have been messing up the house; and when he is a bit older, say eight or nine, his parents may occasionally lure him toward the set so he will not go out and get into trouble in the streets. In a general way, that is what the findings tell us; two-thirds of the parents who have four- to twelve-year-old children claim to impose some controls, "often" or "occasionally," on the timing and content of their children's viewing, especially in the later years. For the younger children, the set is more apt to be used as a baby-sitter.

As one would expect from the previous findings, the level of education of the parents makes a considerable difference in the frequency with which each of the rules is imposed. The parents with more education tend to be stricter (Table 7-22).

The four- to twelve-year-old TV fans have the best chance for happiness with a poorly educated parent. As can be seen from the answers to the first five questions in Table 7-22, the likelihood of having each of the specific rules and regulations applied to children's viewing increases with education of the parents. The child with less-educated parents, is more apt to be actually encouraged to watch in order to keep him occupied.

It seems apparent from these last data on parental control and from other findings throughout the chapter that American parents of different socioeconomic positions have quite divergent conceptions of their roles as guardians over their children's television viewing. In families of higher-educational background the children are sometimes permitted to help in the family decisions about programs to watch when they are viewing together, but not as frequently as in less-educated families. The more-educated parent applies more rules about the amount and content of viewing and less frequently uses the set as a device to keep the children pacified. In general he seems more willing to take action against whatever potential dangers he sees for his children in watching too much or the wrong kinds of programs.

The parents of less-educational background see just as many deleterious effects. If anything, television, with its adult themes and potential for leading children into trouble, is a bit more threatening to them. But

table 7-22

"Here are some things parents have told us they do with their children about TV. Taking just one of your children, do you or your (husband, wife) often, occasionally or never:"

	EDUCATION OF PARENTS			
	Grade School	High School	College	Total
Rules about Viewing Time:				
Set Special Hours For Viewing				
Often	32	45	51	45
Occasionally	19	23	21	22
Never	49	33	28	33
Restrict Amount of Time of Viewing				
Often	28	33	40	34
Occasionally	23	26	28	26
Never	49	41	32	39
Rules about Programs Watched:				
Decide Program Child Watches				
Often	22	28	37	30
Occasionally	27	35	37	35
Never	51	37	26	35
Make Child Change Channel When Program is Objectionable				
Often	30	36	37	35
Occasionally	28	32	40	34
Never	42	32	23	31
Forbid Child to Watch Certain Programs				
Often	17	31	32	30
Occasionally	25	26	27	26
Never	58	43	40	44
Encouragement of Viewing:				
Encourage Child to Watch to Keep Him Occupied				
Often	21	13	7	12
Occasionally	29	27	29	28
Never	50	60	63	60
Encourage Child to Watch to Keep Him at Home				
Often	16	18	2	7
Occasionally	19	13	9	13
Never	65	79	88	80
Base: 100 percent =	(69)	(372)	(178)	(619)

it is in these families that the children have the most influence over the viewing that takes place when the family gets together, and the most autonomy over their own viewing. The less-educated parent thus finds himself in something of a dilemma, with a fair perception of what he does not like his children to see and with a habit of tolerance that prevents him from exercising much control. The decrease in the number of grade school-educated parents who find television's advantages for children outweighing the disadvantages could be the result of a growing frustration among them.

CHAPTER 8

CONCLUSION

In these pages we will take a second glance at some of the findings of the study, concentrating on those few broad themes emerging from the public's response to our questions which would seem to be of particular significance to an understanding of today's television audience: the over-all ten-year change in attitude toward the medium; the social constitution of the audience as it affects reactions to television; the discrepancy between expressed views and viewing behavior; the role of children in family viewing patterns and the new focus of attention on television's journalistic functions. These are the topics on which we will offer a few final comments.

CHANGING ATTITUDES

In the early pages of this report, we found that during the course of a decade television had lost some of the high public regard that Gary Steiner had uncovered in his 1960 survey. The population of viewers in 1970 found television less "satisfying," "relaxing," "exciting," "important," and generally less "wonderful" than had the population of ten years earlier. This decline in regard for television was found among all subgroups of the population. Even the enthusiastic black audience was not quite as en-thusiastic as its brothers and sisters had been ten years before.

The population did not shift its view from one of praise to one of condemnation. No more people were found in 1970 than in 1960 who thought television was downright terrible or just no fun at all. At that end of the attitudinal spectrum, there seems to be a small but consistent number of vilifiers drawn from all segments of the population. Much of the change that took place was rather one of degree, from *summa* to *magna cum laude,* which suggested to us one explanation for the trend. Americans tend to look with great favor on successful technological changes. Some of that consummate praise of 1960 might have been aimed at television-the-marvelous-technological-innovation, a focus that could be expected to recede with the passage of time.

During this same period of declining enthusiasm, as measured by the very unspecific attitude-scale items, some of the responses which the two samples gave to other questions in the interviews were rather dis-quieting to any quick conclusions about a totally turned-off audience. People were watching more television than ever in 1970. Not only that, they seemed to be enjoying more of what they saw. When we turned, for instance, from how people felt *about television* in general to how they *liked the programs they viewed,* on the whole, we found a higher assess-ment of the programs as "somewhat enjoyable" or "extremely enjoyable" than Steiner had found ten years earlier. Probably this apparent contra-diction is explained in part by the "innovation" effect, that would adhere more to the medium in general than to its content. But there is at least one small datum that would suggest an additional interpretation. We asked at a point near the end of the 1970 interviews whether people thought there was more or less variety in television programming than there was ten years before. In response, most people, 70 percent of the sample, said they thought there were more "different kinds of programs." Twenty per-cent said that "things have stayed about the same," and 6 percent thought there were fewer "different kinds of programs." (The rest were undecided.) Unfortunately the query was misplaced, coming after a series of questions about television's altered condition, so the respondents may have been prompted to think about change more than continuity. But if we can believe the responses at all, we might conclude that people were finding more programs among which they could choose than they had before—thus improving the chance that they could watch many things they really enjoyed, even with a diminished respect for television's fare as a whole. Whatever the reason, the public's generalized attitude toward television (as defined by the measures employed in the two studies) *did* decline during the same period of time when much of the content of the medium was picking up new adherents—more people enjoying a larger proportion of the programs, more applause for the performance of the news departments, and broad approval of the changes that were observed over the decade.

THE MASS AUDIENCE AND ITS CONSTITUENTS

It could hardly come as a surprise, even if one had not read the previous study, that people differ in their feelings about television and that some of the differences can be attributed to the viewers' social and economic positions. Such measurable indicators of socioeconomic status as income, occupation, and education, remain among the favorite classification variables among sociologists because they do, indeed, act as good predictors of people's attitudes on a wide range of ideological and substantive issues. In this study, and in Steiner's before it, the respondent's years of formal education was used as the key variable in describing differences among the viewers' feelings about television, in large part because education turns out to be a bit more significant than other variables that might have been substituted, in separating the fans from the critics of the medium.

As we have seen in numerous tables and charts, the better-educated viewers hold the television medium generally in lower esteem; are more inclined to prefer other media as dispensers of news; are apt to be more deliberate in choosing their programs to watch; and are less likely to enjoy what they see. The better-educated viewers also state different preferences for types of television programs—favoring those that provide education and news of the world, preferring "specials" over regular programs, and information over entertainment.

There is no more reason to suspect the educated viewer's expressions of attitude and preference than those of anyone else, but there does seem to be something in the act of television viewing that prevents him from behaving quite as one would predict after listening to him talk. We have seen that he watches the set (by his own admission) just about as much as others during the evening and weekend hours. (Steiner also found very small differences among educational groups in prime-time viewing.) In Minneapolis–St. Paul, we had a more precise test of viewing behavior in the comparisons of diary records and viewer characteristics. The educated viewer distributed his time among program types—comedy, movies, action, information and public affairs, and so forth—in just about the same proportions as did those with less education, and even when he had a clear choice between an information program and some standard entertainment fare, he was just as apt as others to choose the latter.

One is tempted to brand the college-educated viewer as a hypocrite because he does not practice what he preaches, but that would probably be an unjustified interpretation of the findings. It is more likely, in my view, that the college man's expressions of attitude and preference derive, in part, from his notion of television's larger social role; a conception of what *might* be, translated into particular opinions about how television is currently performing and what it should be emphasizing. Much of higher education, after all, is devoted to the detached examination and evaluation of what would otherwise be considered normal and taken for granted; and we would expect of those who have undergone its regimen some ideals of performance, for television and for themselves, beyond the current norms.

There is some evidence that the educated viewers are not at the moment finding in television the content they think should be provided for the public. When we asked about reasons for viewing, it was those with *less* education, not the college educated, who were apt to say they usually watched "because I think I can learn something"—reminiscent of some findings in early radio research. There it was the less educated who sought knowledge in soap operas and quiz shows.[1] It may be fair to say that television is not meeting the educated viewer's standards, and thus he is not expecting to find, and not seeking among its programs the edification he thinks it should provide.

Though education explains more of the variances than anything else in *most* of the attitudes toward television that have been explored in these pages, there are some places where other characteristics of viewers —their sex, age, or race—prove to be of some significance. Men and women, for instance, generally share common views about the medium (and did in 1960 as well) but by 1970 more men than women had left the ranks of the superfans, and more men than women found television no longer "a pleasant way to spend an evening." These are very minor variations in general trends and should serve as no more than a hint that something in the content of television—or something in the lives of men—may have started to create differences between the sexes in views about the medium.

Age, on the other hand, turns out to be a rather powerful predictor of views about one particular type of television content—the programs that deal with social contention—riots, street protests, race problems, campus unrest. Here it is age, regardless of education, that separates the

---

[1] Hertz Herzog, "What Do We Really Know about Daytime Serial Listeners?" in Lazarsfeld and Stanton, eds., *Radio Research, 1942–1943*, New York: Duell, Sloan and Pearce, 1944.

approvers from the disapprovers. The young applaud what the old condemn in what would seem to be expressions about the world at large, attributed to television only as the bearer of bad tidings. Nowhere else in the inquiry do the age groups differ so markedly, but here and there we find just enough variations to test the "generational" and the "life-cycle" theories of how age may affect attitudes, with the cautiously tendered conclusion that attitudes change to conform to the stage of life of the viewers.

It is in the Negro audience that we find the most pronounced deviation from the general average of viewers' attitudes. They are much more enthusiastic about television than any other definable subgroup of the population, and they are more inclined than others to feel that they are not watching as much of it as they would like to. The most surprising finding is that higher education, which exerts a depressing effect on the attitudes of the majority of viewers, seems *not* to dampen the enthusiasm of the Negro audience at all. The better-educated black viewer expresses at least as high a regard for television as the less educated.

The black–white differences, therefore, cannot be explained by attributing to black viewers the values generally associated with lower socioeconomic status. It is more likely that the differences are associated with those traditions that have cut off the black minority, educated or uneducated, from effective participation in many aspects of American life. Television watched at home is one exception—from the beginning, it at least has offered an equal opportunity for vicarious participation in the larger society.

THE VIEWING AUDIENCE

With all these differences in how people feel about television, one could have expected much more variation in the amount of time people spend watching it than was observed in this study or in the study it replicates. The "equal opportunity" measures of evening and weekend viewing, which deliberately handicapped those who have the unfair advantage of being at home during the day, showed a very even spread of viewing among old and young; males and females; college and grade school educated; blacks and whites; wealthy and poor; parents and nonparents; and viewers of different religions, ideologies, and political persuasions. The small variations in viewing levels that occurred were among people who lived in cities of various sizes and in different parts of the country—accidents of geography that have little relationship to *attitudes* about the medium.

The lack of correspondence between determinants of attitudes and viewing behavior, which such findings suggest, leads one away from attempts to explain viewing as a phenomenon associated with socioeconomic status, and toward some more universal explanation. Has television become so psychologically essential that it must be watched the prescribed number of hours a day no matter how much one would like to ignore it, like a hospital meal taken intravenously? Or is it universally useful in the modern world in some more pragmatic sense? Is it a necessity of life, without substitute, for the twentieth-century man who would keep up with the events of the world around him, engage in social intercourse with family and friends without the embarrassment of ignorance, and find easy recourse to needed moments of relaxation? The automobile as a means of getting around would be another modern example of such a necessity. The amount one uses it probably has little to do with how one feels about the appearance of the front grill or about the economic policies of General Motors.

There is also the more mundane possibility that some characteristics of viewers which we have failed to measure *are* significantly associated with television viewing and might have helped to identify the heavy and the light evening and weekend viewers. Perhaps there are differences in people's psychological orientation to real rather than vicarious participation, or significant variations in social disposition toward extramural rather than homebound activities, which would have provided clues as to the meaning of so much television watching in people's lives. Our research has failed to uncover such characteristics, so we are left with an unanswered question.

VIEWING IN THE FAMILY

Our investigation of the role of television in the family setting deals only tangentially with a most important issue at the time of its undertaking. While we are writing this, Senator Pastore's Subcommittee on Communication of the Senate Commerce Committee is considering a report from the Surgeon General's Scientific Advisory Committee on Television and Social Behavior to see what action might be indicated from the results of this research into the effects of television violence on the disposition and actions of young people. All we have seen in our own study are some data on how parents and other adults feel that television has benefited or harmed children and how much control parents say they exercise over their own children's viewing. Such data cannot tell us anything about actual effects, but they can provide some intimation of how well prepared the American public may be to deal with any harmful effects the medium may have.

We find, first of all, that most of the adults in the population (70 percent in 1960 and 76 percent in 1970) feel that children are better off with television than they would be without it, when everything is taken into account, and that this opinion is held more by parents than by non-parents. It is by no means a blanket approval of all television content, but it does suggest that the public would not be prepared to support a national solution such as that imposed by Israel up until 1968, of banning all television from the country.

The reason why most parents find television beneficial in balance is that they see in television a wide variety of educational benefits to their children, from learning words to learning about the world. Some of them see other utility in the medium—to entertain and to keep children occupied —but almost everybody (more than four-fifths of the parents) feels that television *educates*. Most parents also see disadvantages, but without as strong a consensus about their nature. About a third feel that television keeps children from doing other things they should be doing and half find that children are seeing a variety of things they should not—violence, crime, sex, smoking and drinking, things too adult and things that could instill inappropriate moral values. About half of what the parents mention when they talk about television's deleterious content is in the general area of violence, the major theme of Senator Pastore's inquiry; the other half has something to do with broad questions of morality.

Despite the lack of agreement on just what it is about television that may be harmful to children, there are a sufficient number of perceived disadvantages to suggest that parents should want to take action to accentuate the good and restrict the harmful in their children's viewing. But that is where the problem lies—there is something in the structure of American families that diffuses responsibility and inhibits the exercise of authority. The former Prince of Wales is reported to have been impressed, during a visit to this country before the age of television, with how well American parents obey their children. He would find latter-day confirmation of his social insight in some of the data of this study showing the extent to which parents report that their children decide, or help to decide, what programs are to be watched when mothers and children view together or when the whole family gathers around the set. The children come pretty close to being equal partners with their parents in the family decision-making process.

Added to that is the finding that a large proportion of the parents —at least a third of them—tell us that they have no rules about what and when their children watch, when asked the direct question. It is also true that many parents, particularly the better educated, do claim to set viewing hours, decide on programs for their children to watch, or veto certain programs; but in general the data suggest that there are about as many parents in America who look to the children for help in deciding what they (the parents) are going to watch as there are parents who try to decide about their children's viewing.

The family's approach to television viewing may have certain of the virtues of participatory democracy but it also has the drawbacks when it comes to mitigating the effects that watching too much or watching the wrong things—effects that parents themselves perceive—might have on immature minds and ill-formed conceptions of civilized behavior. Parents may be partly lulled by their feeling that television is, in balance, beneficial, partly restrained by their sense of the children's rights in family council, and partly right in their feelings on both scores. But the effect is to leave a large number of children to their own television devices.

CHANGING FOCUS OF ATTENTION

At the beginning of the decade television was seen, predominantly, as an entertainment medium. The critics worried about the low intellectual level of the standard programs, finding the comedy series vacuous and the westerns simplistic and brutal without redeeming social value. They did not see enough on the screen that instructed or edified to alter the general impression of a "vast wasteland." Steiner failed to find much popular support for the critics' indictment among his sample of viewers, but he did find ,that they too were perceiving television as a medium of entertainment. They found it relaxing, not serious; something designed for their enjoyment, not their education. The television personalities they liked best were the stars of entertainment series and the programs they wanted to see again, if they could be rerun, were programs in the "light entertainment" area.

There was a crisis in the life of commercial television just before the 1960 field interviews were conducted that might have served as a harbinger of a new attitude toward television as a medium. The rigged quiz shows of 1958 and 1959 had been exposed, with great publicity before a congressional committee. Confessions had been extracted, dishonesty had been proved, and the industry had been condemned. About three months later, Steiner's interviewers asked people about their reactions to the scandal, with interesting results. A fair number—17 percent of the sample—did not remember anything about it. Among those who could recall the scandal a few (4 percent of the sample) agreed with the statement that "these shocking disclosures show just how bad television is." A larger number chose the statement "no one can really be in favor of this kind of thing, but there's nothing very wrong about it either" (12 percent) or "What happened is a normal part of show business and is perfectly all right" (6 percent). The majority (60 percent) took a middle position: "These practices are very wrong and should be stopped, but you can't condemn all of television because of them." In balance, it was not the strongly condemnatory position that the facts might have justified.

I think the tolerance shown by many of the respondents may have stemmed from their view of television as entertainment—with quiz shows, along with the rest of TV's fare, appropriately judged by their ability to capture the imagination and generate a half hour's worth of excitement— and inappropriately judged by the standards of a college entrance examination. But the congressmen were indeed introducing the criteria of integrity and candor that are normally applied more to the academy and the public office holder than to Broadway, and in television, more to its journalistic than to its entertainment fare.

Since those events, changes have occurred that make the new criteria rather more applicable. According to our tabulations of unduplicated minutes of programming available in two cities, the major relative increase since 1960 came in the areas of news, information, and public affairs. Combined, these areas made up 13 percent of the viewers' menu in 1960 and 24 percent in 1970. That in itself is indicative of a shift in the industry's attention away from entertainment. More important, however, for a study which deals only with people's *perceptions* of reality, is the evidence scattered throughout the responses to our interviewers' questions of a shift in the popular view of television associated with its new role as a journalistic medium.

We see it first in the answers to questions about television's performance compared to other media. In 1960 the choices were mixed, but by 1970 television dominated the answers to these questions even to the point of receiving the most votes as the medium that puts the greatest emphasis on the bad things going on in America *and* as the one that puts the most emphasis on the good things. Later, when we asked people to recall "their biggest moment on television," most of them remembered either space shots or the coverage of President Kennedy's assassination; ten years before they were apt to remember exciting episodes in entertainment features. And when we asked what people thought were the important changes over the decade, news and information programming was mentioned more frequently than other types of television content.

References to television news coverage also crept into the answers to many other questions, even those which were not designed to evoke thoughts about particular types of programs. We asked about some of the advantages of television for children, and among the educational benefits which people saw, was the children's chance to find out what was going on in the world. We asked about disadvantages, and about the same number of adults as in 1960 were worried about violence; but now, unlike 1960, the portrayals of violence which many of them mentioned were the crimes, riots, and wars covered by television news cameras. And among the "technical" changes which people said they had observed, many references were made to the rapid transmission of information from far-away places, including outer space.

It should not be assumed from this, that the American television audience has changed in ten years from a population of entertainment fans to a population of news hawks. Entertainment still dominates the daily offerings and commands most of the viewers' time. But there is apparently a general shift in people's perception of what television is and what it means to them, and the new focus on the news and information content of television has undoubtedly altered people's views about various other aspects of the medium's role—from how it affects the twelve-year-old to whether it is a benign or malevolent force in society.

The occasions which prompt television's news and information pro-gramming could be happy ones conducive to friendly feelings about the world and toward the messenger who brings its news. Or they could be the opposite. The television audience of the late 1960s saw a great deal of the world. They toured any number of American college campuses. They saw the Suez Canal, the Sinai Desert, and the Gulf of Aqaba. They caught glimpses of the temples of the Hué and Angkor Wat, and spent some time watching in the hills of Vietnam and the villages of Biafra. They saw parts of Memphis, Washington, Detroit, Newark, Los Angeles, Buda-pest, Khartoum and the foothills in Peru, and the moon. The travel may have produced broadening effects, but more often than not it was also distressing, featuring the locales of earthquakes, riots, assassinations, and wars. The public has been taken on these frequently unpleasant journeys by television news teams, who, like soldiers and roving diplomats, seem to have had bad travel agents during the past decade or two.

There are some hints as to the way the focus on the news may have affected views about television. The only change in television among the fourteen listed for the respondents which most of them thought was a "change for the worse" was "more live coverage of disruptions in the U. S., like riots and protests in the streets." News has become part of what parents both like and dislike about television for their children. Every-body applauds the advanced technology that permits the coverage of events on earth and in space, but the products of the technology may already have dampened some of the high enthusiasm of people's conversation about television in the days of Steiner's study. But beyond that, the journalistic emphasis may have introduced important new criteria by which television will be judged in the future.

1970 SAMPLING AND FIELD WORK PROCEDURES

Field work for our study was conducted by the Roper Organization among a nationwide cross section of adults, 18 years of age and older, living in households in the continental United States. The following description was prepared by the Roper Organization:

The selection of respondents was determined by probability sampling. The Roper nationwide probability sample of counties and location within counties was used for the distribution of interviews for geographic section and size of place. This probability sample was originally based on 1960 census data, but it has been updated as much as possible in accordance with sales management and recent census estimates to take into account population changes since 1960. In cities of 50,000 population and over, blocks were drawn at random proportionate to population as reported in the 1960 census. However, to take into account possible changes since 1960, zero blocks as of 1960 were also drawn and examined. Addresses of households on both sets of blocks (those populated in 1960 and zero blocks now populated) were prelisted. Based on these prelistings, sampling rates for each block selected for inclusion in the sample were computed and specific households selected in random manner for inclusion in the sample. In places of under 50,000 population for which no block statistics are available, routes were randomly selected from maps and a system of simultaneous listing of households was used, with every *n*th household designated for inclusion in the sample.

Each designated household was specifically assigned as either a male or female household. Within these designated households, family members (either male or female according to assignment) 18 years of age and older were listed from oldest to youngest, and a random system used to select the designated respondent. Only one member per household was interviewed.

Because of our special interest in young people 18- and 19-years old, an oversampling of interviews was made among this age group. This was done by assigning an extra interview for persons in this age group to every nth block or route, and the interviewers were instructed to "find" an 18- or 19-year-old respondent living on or close to the assigned block or route. Thus, while this procedure is a departure from the probability method, it provides a good spread of interviews.

The basic sample size was 2957 households, anticipating a yield of 2000 interviews. This figure was arrived at by estimating the number of households that would qualify for having family members of the right sex (one or more males in a household designated for male interviewing and one or more females in households designated for female interviewing), plus figuring on a 75 percent completion rate among designated respondents in qualifying households.

This 75 percent completion rate was not realized. Interviewers had been required to make up to four attempts at different times of day (or on different days) to obtain an interview at each designated household, except for final refusals encountered before the fourth call. An examination of the call records found a number of cases where the designated respondent was not at home at the time of the fourth call, and it looked as though further calls might produce an interview. Therefore, to increase the yield, up to four additional calls were later made at 215 households in those places where the completion rate had been relatively low. Both operations (the regular interviewing plus the extra call backs) resulted in completed interviews with 70 percent of the designated respondents.

In making their introductions to respondents, interviewers stated the purpose of the survey as shown at the top of the first page of the questionnaire. No respondent was told that the subject of the study was television until the answers to Question 3 had been completed in order not to bias the answers to the first three questions, which compared television with other products and media.

The interviewing was conducted by regular members of the Roper interviewing staff. Ten percent of each interviewer's work was validated to insure that the interviews were made properly.

The interviewing was conducted during the months of March and April, 1970 (except for the additional call backs which were made in May).

Reasons Why Interviews Were Not Completed with Designated Respondents in the 1970 Study

	Total	Male Households	Female Households
Number not completed in qualifying households	788	383	405
	Percent	Percent	Percent
On the last call made:			
No one at home	21	17	24
Neighbor/postman, etc. reported family away for some time	3	2	4
Designated respondent at home but:			
Refused (not interested, no time, etc.)	27	28	25
Sick	4	3	4
Family member refused for them . . .	2	4	1
Too old	2	1	2
Refused because of length of interview	1	1	1
Deaf	1	1	1
Too busy at the time	1	1	*
Other	2	1	2
"Someone" answered but:			
Refused *any* information	13	13	13
Designated respondent not home . .	5	8	3
Non-English speaking	5	5	5
Designated respondent away for long time	3	2	3
Refused for designated respondent.	2	3	1
Designated respondent in hospital, nursing home	1	1	1
Other	1	1	1
All other:			
Final call not made	3	3	3
Wouldn't come to door	1	1	2
Faulty address	1	1	1
Dangerous looking	1	*	1
Other	2	3	1

* Less than .5 percent.

Completion Rates

	Total number of households assigned	Percentage of households with no one living there of assigned sex	Total number of qualifying households	Percentage of completed interviews in qualifying households
Total	2957	10	2660	70
Male	1527	16	1289	70
Female	1430	4	1371	70
Geographic section				
Northeast	722	9	655	64
Midwest	814	11	728	72
South	927	10	838	74
Far West	494	11	439	70
Size of Place				
Over 1,000,000	250	14	215	56
250,000 to 1,000,000 ..	393	13	343	63
100,000 to 250,000 ...	213	13	186	61
25,000 to 100,000	465	11	416	68
2500 to 25,000	565	12	499	72
Under 2500	175	21	154	81
Open country	715	6	675	80
Urban fringe	181	5	172	66
Economic level				
A	——	—	81	64
B	——	—	622	78
C	——	—	1318	77
D	——	—	385	74
Not recorded	——	—	254	15

These percentages should be read across.

In 16 percent of male households assigned, no male 18 years of age and over lived there.

In 70 percent of qualifying male households, an interview was completed with the designated male respondent.

In 64 percent of qualifying economic-level households, an interview was completed with the designated respondent.

Completion Rates cont.

	Total number of households assigned	Percentage of households with no one living there of assigned sex	Total number of qualifying households	Percentage of completed interviews in qualifying households
Age of designated respondent				
18–24	——	—	237	92
25–34	——	—	416	85
35–39	——	—	674	82
50–64	——	—	539	78
65 & over	——	—	393	79
Not recorded	——	—	401	5

These percentages should be read across.

SAMPLE
AND CENSUS
COMPARISONS

Comparisons of the 1960 and 1970 samples and population data on the major background variables of the study are presented here. The detailed sampling procedure used in 1970 is also reviewed so that the interested reader may evaluate the adequacy of the sampling techniques (Appendix A). Data for the entire U. S. population are based on Bureau of the Census reports of the 1960 and 1970 censuses. The proportions reported in the tables are computed only for those in the population 18-years old and older (unless otherwise indicated) so as to be comparable to the data from the studies, in which only persons 18 and older were interviewed. All 1970 sample proportions are appropriately weighted to take into account the oversampling of the 18–19-year age group. In general, there appears to be a good fit between sample and population data for both studies.

Age (Table 1)—Age distributions appear to closely represent the populations in 1960 and 1970, with the exception of the 20–29-year age category in 1970. For the 1970 sample, 18 percent compared to 22 percent of the population fall into this age category.

Sex (Table 2)—The distribution of males and females in both samples corresponds well to the distribution in the populations. In no case are the sample estimates off more than one percent.

195

table 1
Age (in percentages)

	1960			1970	
	NORC	ROPER	CENSUS	SAMPLE	CENSUS
18–19	4	3	4	5	6
20–29	18	21	19	18	22
30–39	23	22	21	19	17
40–49	19	18	20	20	18
50–59	15	18	16	17	16
60 + ...	20	17	21	22	22

Sources: *Current Population Reports,* Series P–25, No. 441, March 19, 1970; and *General Population Characteristics: U.S. Summary,* Series PC (1)–B1, January 1972.

Education (Table 3)—There appear to be some biases in the distribution of educational groups in both samples. In 1960, the lower educational groups (0–4 and 5–8) are underestimated. In 1970, these same groups are again underestimated but to a much smaller degree. For all other educational groups, the sample proportions closely approximate those in the population.

Income (Table 4)—The sample estimates of income distributions reveal a certain amount of bias. In 1960, those earning less than $3,000, and those earning more than $5,000 are underrepresented, although the large number of "no responses" for the income question in this survey may account for the discrepancy. The 1970 survey shows an overrepre-

table 2
Sex (in percentages)

	1960			1970	
	NORC	ROPER	CENSUS	SAMPLE	CENSUS
Males	48	50	50	48	48
Females	52	50	50	52	53

Sources: *Current Population Reports,* Series P-25, No. 441, March 19, 1970; and *General Population Characteristics: U.S. Summary,* Series PC(1)–B1, January 1972.

table 3
Education (in percentages)

| | 1960 | | | 1970 | |
	NORC	ROPER	CENSUS	SAMPLE (Re-spondent)	CENSUS
0–4	4	2	8	3	4
5–8	23	22	29	16	19
9–11	23	21	20	19	18
12	25	31	27	36	36
1–2 college	9	9	8	12	12
3–4 college	8	8	9	14	12

Source: *Statistical Abstracts*, 1970.

sentation of those earning between $7,000–$9,000 while the highest income group is underrepresented.

    Occupation (Table 5)—Comparisons of sample occupational groups dichotomized by white-blue collar occupations show a high correspondence of respondents' occupations with gross census categorizations.

table 4
Income (in percentages)

DISTRIBUTION OF FAMILIES	1960			1970	
	NORC*	ROPER**	CENSUS	SAMPLE	CENSUS
Under $3,000	20	17	22	12	10
3,000–4,999	24	23	20	10	10
5,000–6,999	24	19	24	12	12
7,000–9,999	15	16	20	27	21
10,000 & over ...	10	8	14	38	47

  * Five percent no response.
  ** Seventeen percent no response.
    Sources: *Statistical Abstracts*, 1970; and *General Social and Economic Characteristics: U. S. Summary*, Series PC(1)–C1, January 1972.

table 5
Occupation (in percentages)

| | 1960 | | | | 1970 | | | |
| | NORC | | ROPER | | CENSUS* | | SAMPLE | CENSUS** |
	Respondent	Spouse	Respondent	Spouse		Respondent	Spouse	
White collar	39	33	43	37	43	47	40	49
Blue collar	52	46	47	47	56	53	60	51
NA	10	21	10	15	—	—	—	—

* Employed persons 14-years old and over.
** Employed persons 16-years old and over.
Source: *Statistical Abstracts*, 1970.

It should be noted that 1960 census figures are based on persons 14-years old and older, and 1970 figures are based on persons 16-years old and older, which probably overweighs the census figures in the blue-collar category somewhat, since the sample data include only 18-year olds and over.

Race (Table 6)—Sample racial distributions appear to be quite representative of such distributions in the population.

Geographical Distribution (Table 7)—In both the 1960 and 1970

table 6
Race (in percentages)

| | 1960 | | | 1970 | |
	NORC	ROPER	CENSUS	SAMPLE	CENSUS
Negro	10	12	9	10	10
White	89	86	90	89	89
Other	—	—	1	1	1
NA	1	2	—	—	—

Source: *Current Population Reports*, Series P–25, No. 441, December 19, 1970.

table 7
Geographical Distribution (in percentages)

| | 1960 | | | 1970 | |
	NORC	ROPER	CENSUS*	SAMPLE	CENSUS*
New England	4	9	6	5	6
Middle Atlantic ..	23	17	19	17	18
E N Central	19	21	20	20	20
W N Central	10	9	9	8	8
S Atlantic	13	13	14	15	15
E S Central	6	8	7	8	6
W S Central	10	9	9	10	10
Mountain	4	3	4	5	4
Pacific	11	10	12	12	13

* Total population.
Source: *Statistical Abstracts*, 1970; and *General Population Characteristics: U. S. Summary*, Series PC(1)–B1, January 1972.

THE NEGRO SAMPLE

table 8
Education (Negro)

EDUCATION	1970 SAMPLE	MARCH 1970 CENSUS SURVEY
0–4	13	12
5–6	22	24
7–8	—	—
9–11	29	25
12	22	27
1–2 College	7	7
3–4 plus	6	5

Source: *Current Population Report*, Series P–20, No. 207, November 1970.

samples, the estimates of the geographical distributions of the population closely approximate the figures presented by the census, all regions of the country being adequately represented.

While it is felt that both samples provide a reasonably good proportion to population data, the two samples have not completely avoided certain biases in the distribution of some population characteristics. The major discrepancies in the 1970 sample seem to be the underrepresentation of the 20–29-year-old age group, the lower educational groups, and highest income group; in the 1960 sample, the lower-educational and the lowest- and middle-income groups are underrepresented.

The Negro Sample (Tables 8 and 9)—The 194 blacks in the 1970 sample are compared with the U.S. population of Negroes in these two tables. There is a fairly close correspondence in years of schooling, with some underrepresentation of high school graduates in the sample. The age and sex comparisons in Table 9 show greater discrepancies. In the sample there are too few young males, too many old males, and too few old (60 +) females.

table 9
Age and Sex

	SAMPLE	1970 CENSUS
BLACK MALES		
18–19	3	3
20–29	5	12
30–39	8	9
40–49	9	8
50–59	9	7
60+	17	8
BLACK FEMALES		
18–19	3	3
20–29	12	13
30–39	11	10
40–49	8	10
50–59	11	8
60+	6	10

Source: *General Population Characteristics: U.S. Summary*, Series PC(1)–B1, January 1972.

A STATISTICAL NOTE

Since the body of the report is rather skimpy in its methodological discussion, we are adding these brief descriptions of some of the procedures employed in data analysis and of the means by which estimates of statistical confidence limits may be derived.

TABULAR PRESENTATION

The percentages found in the various tables and charts in this report are based on the number of cases in a cell *excluding* "no answers" to the questions involved, unless there is an indication to the contrary. For this reason the base for the percentages which are given will vary from table to table depending on the number of "no answers."

Another reason for minor discrepancies in the number of cases indicated stems from the 1970 oversampling of 18- and 19-year-olds. When properly weighted, each of the answers of people in this age group are counted half. If a tabulation indicated 356.5 people answered a question in a certain way, it would be rounded to 357 cases. Where tables are broken by age, so that the teen-agers are treated separately, the total unweighted number of 18–19-year olds is presented.

AID

A computer program called Automatic Interaction Detection (AID) was employed at several points in our analysis of the 1960 and 1970 data. The program is designed to take into account the interrelationships of several independent, or predictor, variables and indicate the extent to which each of them contribute to an explanation of one dependent, or criterion, variable (in our case attitude toward television, amount of viewing, and planned viewing). The program proceeds by dichotomizing each predictor variable, selecting the one that serves as the best predictor when the interrelationships with the others are determined, and then continuing similarly with the other variables. For a full description of this technique, see John A. Sonquist, *Multivariate Model Building*, Ann Arbor: Institute of Social Research, 1970.

COHORT ANALYSIS MEASURE

The test of the generational and life-cycle theories in Chapter 3 assumes that the over-all, ten-year trend as expressed in the marginal percentages should be taken into account. We would argue that this over-all trend potentially affects all the individual ten-year differences within age groups or age cohorts equally, so these latter differences should be adjusted by subtracting the trend figures. (This is comparable to measuring the height of waves breaking up on a beach by taking the height of the tide as the base from which they start.)

The "mean of horizontal variations less trend" is derived by subtracting the trend figure (the 1960–1970 difference for the total samples) from each horizontal difference (e.g., the 1960 18–19-year-olds versus the 1970 18–19-year-olds) and computing a mean for the results. A perfect support of the life-cycle interpretation would result in a figure of zero. Similarly with the diagonal differences, with a perfect support of the generational interpretation being a resulting figure of zero.

MEASURING THE MENU

In comparing the 1960 and the 1970 TV menu (the types of programs being broadcast), and in the comparisons of menu with diet (the programs watched), we used *unduplicated minutes* as our menu measure. This meant that if two programs of the same type, that is, two half-hour "action" programs, appeared at the same time only 30 minutes of "action" programming was recorded in our tabulations. Two other measures might have been used, and were used by Steiner—the number of minutes devoted to programs in the various types, whether duplicated by others or not and the number of programs, regardless of length or duplication. We think that unduplicated minutes allow for more valid comparisons of diet versus menu since it is difficult for a viewer to watch two action programs simultaneously; he has to choose one of them in competition with a program of some other type.

SAMPLING ERROR

In the body of this report we have not given estimates of confidence intervals for the various results. The establishment of such estimates is complicated by the fact that the data reported are derived from three sample surveys (two in 1960 which were subsequently combined and one in 1970) which used similar but not identical multistage area-probability sampling procedures.

For the reader who is interested in a rough estimate, at best, for 95 percent confidence intervals for proportions, we suggest the following: Assume that we are dealing with two samples, 1960 (N=2400) and 1970 (N=1900). Furthermore, assume that each was obtained by use of simple random-sampling procedures. Following the rules of thumb suggested for clustered sampling by Leslie Kish, *Survey Sampling*, New York: John Wiley and Sons, 1957, multiply each derived confidence interval by 1.7. The resulting values are shown in the following table:

95 Percent **Confidence Intervals** (in percentage)

PROPORTION NEAR	1960 Sample	1970 Sample
90	2	2
80	3	3
70	3	4
60	3	4
50	3	4
40	3	4
30	3	4
20	3	3
10	2	2

The use of this table is best shown by an example. Suppose that the percentage of respondents manifesting characteristic X for the 1970 sample is 62 percent. Locate the line corresponding to 60 percent and the entry for the 1970 sample. As a rough estimate we could expect that chances are 95 out of 100 that the population percentage lies between 58 percent (i.e., 62 — 4 percent) and 66 percent (i.e., 62 + 4 percent).

SIGNIFICANCE OF DIFFERENCES BETWEEN PERCENTAGES

A similarly rough calculation can be made for estimating the statistical significance of the differences between percentages found in the various tables and charts. The following table is adapted from Kish, *Survey Sampling*. The estimates are on the conservative side:

Sampling Errors of Differences between Percentages

Number of Cases	Number of Cases						
	2000	1000	700	500	400	300	200
FOR PERCENTAGES FROM 35 TO 65							
2000	4	5	6	7	7	8	9
1000		6	6	7	8	8	10
700			7	8	8	9	10
500				8	9	9	10
400					9	10	11
300						10	11
200							12
FOR PERCENTAGES AROUND 20 AND 80							
2000	3	4	5	5	6	6	8
1000		5	5	6	6	7	8
700			6	6	6	7	8
500				7	7	7	9
400					7	8	9
300						8	9
200							10

As an example of the use of this table we might assume that we are comparing a percentage figure somewhere in the 35 to 65 percent range on about 300 cases with another percentage based on about 200 cases. We would need a difference of at least 11 percentage points to be fairly certain that the difference is meaningful and not a result of sampling error.